Michael Wilding | Wild & Woolley: A Publishing Memoir

Michael Wilding

GIRAMONDO

Wild & Woolley | A Publishing Memoir

First published 2011
from the Writing & Society Research Group
at the University of Western Sydney
by the Giramondo Publishing Company
PO Box 752
Artarmon NSW 1570 Australia
www.giramondopublishing.com

Designed by Harry Williamson
Typeset by Andrew Davies
in 10/14.5 pt Minion Pro
Printed and bound by Ligare Book Printers
Distributed in Australia by NewSouth Books

National Library of Australia
Cataloguing-in-Publication data:

Wilding, Michael
Wild & Woolley: A Publishing Memoir

ISBN 978-1-920882-74-7

809

To Pat Woolley

I met Pat Woolley at a performance event in the inner-city Sydney suburb of Broadway, one of those performances where the performers took off their upper garments and exchanged them with each other, so there were bare breasts along with the changing and singing, which in 1973 was considered the height of the *avant-garde*. Robyn Ravlich and Aleks Danko presented a piece called 'The Path of Poetry' and Tim Burns filled up the stairway with Styrofoam. People had to crawl over it to get downstairs. Pat and I went back to my place in Balmain where the poets had already entered through the bathroom window and were sitting around writing poems on my typewriter and eating and drinking whatever they could find, which wouldn't have been a lot, since I ate out most of the time and drank in the pub. Robert Adamson, John Forbes, Laurie Duggan and Nigel Roberts as I remember, give or take a few.

'I want to start a publishing company one day called Wild and Woolley,' Pat said as we sat in some pub or restaurant a couple of days later.

'Do you know my name?' I asked.

'No,' she said, not especially interested.

I am not sure she even asked what it was. But I told her.

'I am the Wild to your Woolley,' I said. Maybe. Maybe not as epigrammatically.

I had been wanting to start a publishing house for a while, even though I now had a publisher, Frank Thompson at University of Queensland Press, who was publishing my fiction. I liked the idea of a small press, I liked books. Magazines I had edited. Indeed I was still editing one, *Tabloid Story*. *Tabloid Story* was a short story magazine that Frank Moorhouse, Carmel Kelly and I had established in 1972. It was produced as a supplement to existing magazines and weeklies, using their tabloid newspaper format, and their circulations of 40,000 to 100,000 copies, to promote short fiction beyond the 500 to 2000 copies of the traditional literary quarterlies.

But with magazines there was always that remorseless time factor, getting out the next issue, no respite, and then the previous issue was out of date and deemed unsaleable. Books could come out in their own time, no pressures. And they would be permanent. Eternal.

Pat knew about alternative publishing. Before coming to Australia she had distributed the *LA Free Press*, that font and origin of the underground press in Los Angeles that we had all heard about but probably never seen. Coming to Australia, she had started Tomato Press in Melbourne, and published a collection of Pamela Brown's poems. Now she had moved the printing press and plate-maker to

Sydney and had a printery in Glebe. Tomato Press had something of an underground and feminist agenda. Tomatoes were what Americans called girls in those days. Some Americans. And the underground, the alternative, was, like performance art, the cutting edge of the new.

This was a moment of technological shift, the introduction of offset printing, replacing the old hot-metal and monotype machines. Well, offset had been around for a dozen years or more; as an undergraduate at Oxford I had experimented with it when it first came in, producing a parodic colour-supplement in *Isis*. But now it was wide-spread. And now IBM had introduced their Selectric Composer machine, a glorified typewriter. But oh, how glorified! You could put in a different golf ball for different fonts. And you could justify. Not that in the radical seventies you necessarily felt the need for justification.

So Wild & Woolley was conceived, though not born. Pat was leaving Australia, returning to California via Greece and London. Ah well!

She wrote to me from London where she had got herself a job on *Private Eye* magazine and volunteered at *Oz,* appearing on the famous naked cover of the last issue with Felix Dennis and others. Auberon Waugh came into *Private Eye* the first week she was there to dictate his column. She couldn't understand his accent so told him, 'Just leave the copy, I'll be able to read it.' He never noticed any changes. She sent me letters written on the composing machine, one column unjustified, the other column the same text justified at the press of a button. The technology was out there waiting for us and Pat could use it.

At the end of 1973 I flew to Los Angeles and joined Pat there. She got a rubber stamp made and bought some index cards. We made our own business cards: Wild & Woolley Publishers & Distributors. People looked at them in stunned amazement.

'Neat,' they said, in the way Californians said it.

Or, maybe, 'Like, neat.'

Then we borrowed her father's van and drove up the coast highway through Big Sur to San Francisco and visited City Lights and told them their books were hard to get in Australia and we would be their agent.

Lawrence Ferlinghetti smiled encouragingly, took a walking stick from beneath the packing bench and hitched down a bowler hat from its hook on the wall and put it on and we got ourselves photographed with him. Later I realised the hat and stick were memorabilia from Charlie Chaplin's movie *City Lights*, or replicas thereof; at the time I thought it was just some bizarre fancy dress affectation.

Ferlinghetti said Commonwealth distribution was handled from London by McBride and Broadley but he would have a word with them. A couple of months later back in Sydney we received an order from a bookshop to supply a couple of City Lights titles. We were amazed.

We asked a lawyer I knew from drinking with the Sydney Push at the Newcastle Hotel to draw up the legal documents to make us into a company. Morrie Isaacs was primarily a divorce lawyer, but he did it all the same. We were in business.

Years later McBride and Broadley went bust, and Dick McBride came out to Australia where his wife was teaching at Southport on the Gold Coast. Years after that I met him back in my home town in England in a branch of the booksellers, Waterstones. He was soon afterwards sacked. 'Is this old fart wearing a beanie the image we want?' the manager asked. It was cold in winter in Worcester so no wonder he wore a beanie. Nonetheless they sacked him. So much for the literary heritage: a man who had sold books at the City Lights shop in San Francisco, a man Kerouac used to phone up for drunken conversations late at night, a man who wrote a memoir of Ginsberg – Ginsberg who had been responsible for advising Ferlinghetti to cut off credit to McBride and Broadley, so pushing them into bankruptcy, he told me. In the mid-1990s Dick published the UK edition of a selection of my stories, *Somewhere New*, with his press McBride's Books.

There was considerable cultural optimism around in the early 1970s. Even before the Liberal-Country Party coalition bowed out after twenty-three years in 1972, it had expanded the activities of the old Commonwealth Literary Fund. Censorship was being relaxed. There was a backlog of cultural production waiting to appear. Those twenty-three years may have been repressive and conformist, but beneath the surface things had been bubbling and now they began to burst forth. It was this release of the pent-up, rather than any new creative impulse, that characterised those brief years of the Labor government.

And a release from all the anti-war protests that had taken up so much time and energy and emotion. I wanted to return to literature, move on from the political, move on from all those meetings, marches, protests, petitions, harangues. They had been a necessary activity, but now we could return to what life should properly be about: writing, reading, and the arithmetic of publishing. All those readings against the war in Vietnam we had so busily organised had helped establish an audience for current writing. Now it was time to move from appearance and performance into the permanency of print.

Publishing was one of the areas that had been bottled up. Maybe it always is. Then, as now, Australian publishing was mainly the business of overseas-owned corporations, British primarily at this time, multinationals not yet having fully emerged. There were only a dozen or so Australian novels being published in any given year. The publishers primarily imported books written, printed and published in some foreign field. We would redress the balance. It was not only a cultural mission, it was also an opportunity to publish what the established publishers neglected. There was no shortage of product, as we soon learned to call the material of our trade.

In the midst of the English revolution, Sir Thomas Browne complained of the tyranny of the press, of printing. He wrote from a royalist perspective. For the puritans and sectarians and radicals and republicans, the press had been the great liberating weapon of revolution. With the breakdown of censorship, the press had been the weapon that had disseminated alternative ideas, new social possibilities, visions of a different future.

And for a pacifist, or anti-war activist as pacifists came to be more aggressively termed, books were a cleaner-handed weapon than guns or knives or explosives.

So, publishing had a lot going for it. Publishing involved collaborative work, the rewards of community. It was a salvation from isolation. It had physical, tactile satisfactions. And you could do it. You did not have to find backers or angels or bank debt as filmmakers and theatre producers had to. You did not have to acquire a government licence as radio and television broadcasting required. A quite amazing number of people used to ask me when we began Wild & Woolley, can anyone just start publishing? Shades of the controlled society, that such a question should have been so frequently asked.

Writing can be a very lonely occupation. Just sitting there, pen in hand, or keyboard before you. Painters seem to be able to paint while holding conversations. Writers need the silence and isolation, usually. Some writers have sought community in public appearances. Dickens famously did his series of readings to huge audiences, as well as taking part in amateur and semi-professional theatre. But theatre, readings, performance, radio, I always found too transitory, too ephemeral to be ultimately satisfying. What was there to show for it at the end? In that regard lecturing and tutoring were similar. The pleasures, if any, were those of performance, and I had a suspicion of performance. Performance in lectures, I suspected, was something in inverse proportion to truth and content. There were colleagues of mine at the university who enjoyed it – performing, holding forth, speaking on the radio. I had inherited a puritan suspicion of all that theatrical stuff. And I had inherited a concomitant privileging of the written word and the book. Even newspapers were too transitory. And alienated. You got to see your name appear, but there was never much human contact, it was all done by mail or phone or, now, email. One of the advantages of living in Australia for a serious writer was that freelance journalism paid so badly that it was never much of a temptation, hardly worth doing. It was rarely something that made one of those offers you could not refuse that would drag you away from the books you should have been writing, as it clearly was in the UK or USA.

But publishing was different. The ineffable pleasure of messing about with books. They were physical, tactile, satisfyingly solid. They had their aesthetic appeals, the design, the typography, the smells of ink and paper, all the satisfactions of the resulting physical objects. Thousands of them. And there was the further great delight of publishing. The pleasure of bypassing the traditional gatekeepers and controllers, the possibility of ignoring all the vetting and editing by the class and economic and political and other gangs that controlled the business. Why compromise and deal with them? Why not just do your own thing? This was the 1970s.

The point was not, for me, to make money. The point was to publish books that were worthwhile, and not to lose money. It is another way of doing it. An alternative to the commercial. There used to be a number of other possibilities than the commercial. The university used to be one, a repository of culture and learning. Art used to be another. Even commercial publishing used to believe in using some of the profits from publishing money-making books to subsidise the non-money-making: recognising that there were books worth publishing that were not, at least in the immediate instance, likely to make money. But were worth doing.

It is an attitude that has changed, along with other changes in business practice. Now the ideology of free-market capitalism is that everything should pay its way. Art and universities included. And only things that make money are worth doing. But this is not the place to launch into a critique of late-capitalist practice. The point is simply that there have been alternative models that co-existed with commercial culture. And Wild & Woolley followed one of them.

Robert Adamson had published a volume of poems, *Canticles on the Skin* in 1970, and he also had a prose work, *Zimmer's Essay*. It was an account of his prison experiences, co-written in some unexplained way with Bruce Hanford. Bruce Hanford was reputedly an American draft-dodger who had married the daughter of an Australian Army general. He was involved in a so-called alternative paper, *The Digger*. *The Digger* was said to be named after Rupert Murdoch's sobriquet, 'the Dirty Digger'; *Zimmer's Essay* was named after and cut-down from Bob Dylan's birth-name, Zimmerman. Adamson was an early Dylanologist. Reputedly again Bruce had locked Adamson in a room to get him to complete the manuscript. Back in prison again. But that same story was told about Marcus Clarke when he was writing *His Natural Life* a hundred years earlier. It went with the territory. Prison novels. *Zimmer's Essay* was never quite finished but Hanford serialised what there was of it in *The Digger*. I suggested to Bob we publish it as a book. He agreed and gave me the typescript, something of a mess, bits of Bob's reminiscences together with a brief history of penology by Bruce. I juggled the bits and pieces around to give it some sort of coherence and shape and devised chapter breaks. It still came in short, so we bulked it out with a selection of Bob's prison poems, prison poems being all the rage in those heady days. There were prison poets and prison playwrights emerging everywhere. But Adamson was the first of them, and the one who endured. And this was his first memoir, though in the ensuing years he wrote a couple more volumes of true confessions covering his early years.

Vicki Viidikas had published a collection of poems, *Condition Red*, with the University of Queensland Press in 1973. The original manuscript was voluminous. She was always a prolific writer. It had to be cut and reduced to suit their Paperback Poets series format, and with much agony and exasperation this was done. In desperation at UQP's request for her to select no more than fifty pages from her typescript of two hundred or more poems, she had turned to me for help. Or maybe I had offered it unsolicited. Anyway, whichever, I made a selection.

Condition Red made an immediate impact. I now proposed making a similar selection of stories from her battered cardboard suitcase full of manuscripts, and she agreed. *Wrappings*, she insisted on calling it. We tried to tell her it was not the sort of title that would attract purchasers and result in massive sales. But she was adamant, in this as in so much else. *Wrappings* was a powerful volume that gave memorable voice to the anguishes and ecstasies of her encounters with the world. She was a fiction writer of genius. 'The realities of a woman's life,' the USA *Small Press Review* described it. This was before women's writing had become a part of the literary agenda of Australia. In this, as in her technical experiments, she was a true innovator. Two more collections of her poetry followed, *Knabel* from Wild & Woolley in 1978 – another impossible title, but she was adamant again – and *India Ink* from Hale & Iremonger in 1984.

Vicki was one of the most brilliant talents of the reawakened Australian literary scene of the late 1960s and 70s. She blazed through the inner-city worlds of Balmain and East Sydney, and the alternative settlements of the NSW coast, with an unforgettable intensity. She wrote directly from experience and her whole life was a commitment to seeking out experience, to capturing the authentic. Her stories and poems embodied the mood of that heady moment of creativity, and gave expression in a unique and direct idiom to what so many of her contemporaries felt. 'Her writing is strong and honest, and she needs no tricks or games,' wrote Anne Summers.

Born in Australia of an Estonian father and an Australian mother, and claiming descent from Ned Kelly's family, she left school at 15. She worked at a series of casual jobs and was married for a time to the painter Bob Finlayson. In the 1970s she received some support from Literature Board fellowships. Balmain in the late 1960s and early 70s was home to a horde of writers and publications. Vicki was a striking, effervescent figure around the pubs, the parties and the waterfront readings of those years. Her poems appeared in Nigel Roberts's *Free Poetry*, in Robert Adamson's *New Poetry*, and in Tom Shapcott's anthology *Australian Poetry Now*, and her stories in *Tabloid Story* and *Stand*.

For Vicki life and writing were inextricable. She spun her writing out of the life she lived. She wrote and travelled endlessly, up and down the coast of Australia from Melbourne to Mullumbimby, through Thailand,

India, Israel, England, France and Greece. In part it was the hippy trail, an ongoing search for experience, excess and enlightenment. She empathised with the varieties of religious experience she encountered, while remaining detached. She did a lot of drugs. She followed the path of the wandering troubadour. It is an honourable tradition. Arguably, it is the true tradition.

This makes it sound too abstract. Vicki's writing was always vivid and precise, focusing on the telling detail, on the sharp-eyed observation. From the control-freak cocaine dealer in his waterside apartment to the menacing yet alluring Indian monkey-man, she could summon up situations of extraordinary power and subtlety.

Like the great jazz singers she so admired, Bessie Smith and Billie Holiday, Vicki's voice is always recognisable, always effortless. There is nothing that sounds rehearsed or over-produced. She aimed for spontaneity. 'Trying to catch the voice' she called one piece. To call her a stylist is misleading – or so she would no doubt have thought. Her whole project was to be free of affectation, of manner, of precedent. But her clarity, her directness, her visionary evocations and surreal connections have the characteristic note of an assured, spare, vividly colourful modernism. You do not achieve spontaneity like Vicki's without years of commitment.

Vicki emerged as a writer in the late 1960s. She chronicled the era of what seemed at the time like liberation, one of the first to record the sexual and drug revolution. She eagerly seized the opportunity to record what had rarely been written about explicitly before, a world of sex and drugs, gays, lesbians, prostitutes, rapists and their victims, drug-dealers and their junky clients. These are sketches from the life, not narratives manufactured for commercial gain or propagandist agenda. Vicki presented no agenda: other than the agenda of the clear-eyed writer, the Isherwood 'I am a camera'. There were precedents, of course: Rimbaud, Anna Kavan, LeRoi Jones, and she knew their work. Like every serious writer, she read widely and intensely. She follows on from D. H. Lawrence in her portrayal of the crackling tensions of male–female relationships. She vividly portrays a remorseless parade of unsatisfactory men, and the casual pick-ups after a party in Sydney or a carnival in Paris.

Thirty-five years after they were written, her searing attacks on male self-involvement and overall unsatisfactoriness still make me flinch. No doubt they should, since a couple were written at me. Not written for me, or to me, but confrontationally at me. Writing was part of an ongoing dialogue with the world for Vicki and other writers of the 1970s. Pre-dating blogs and the web, it was a direct and instant medium of exchange, inviting rapid reaction. We used to respond to each other's stories and poems with stories and poems in reply. It was not a matter of manufacturing a product and marketing it. Of course, some were doing that and have been most successful. But that was a world for which Vicki had nothing but scorn.

What should have been a significant literary career failed to eventuate. It was not that she ceased to write. She continued to write voluminously, producing stories and poems, and an amazing novel, *Kali and the Dung Beetle*, that ranged from Sydney in the 70s to India in the 80s. But the world of publishers and editors found her difficult, and she in turn found them contemptible. She remained true to her art, refused to compromise, continued to write, but except for rare appearances in magazines and anthologies, effectively ceased to publish. It is a tragedy and a scandal that so comparatively small a part of her work appeared in print. She remained adamant in her refusal of the comfortable and the conventional. As Christina Stead recognised, Vicki took chances. In that time-honoured tradition of the *avant-garde* artist, she preferred bohemia to bourgeois existence, and she preferred the demi-monde to bohemia. In her last years – and she was only 50 when she died – she became a myth, lost to the view of the literary world that she had inspired, stimulated, informed and reviled.

Wrappings and *Zimmer's Essay* came out in hardback in 1974 in a run of 750 copies each. They were both short books. This we quickly perceived as no bad thing. Many of the early Wild & Woolley titles were short. They cost us less to print, but we could still sell them at the usual going price for new books. We had no way of achieving economies of scale by printing 25,000 copies of these titles, no way of moving that number with our distribution. We were not large or established enough to obtain preferential printing and trucking contracts. And our readers probably preferred short books: these were the days of dope and distraction, before the onset of the commercial blockbuster.

Initially we had decided on publishing in hard cover. We could charge a higher retail price, achieve a better margin, and cover our costs. Maybe, we dreamed, we could sell on paperback rights to a paperback house. We were not without strategies. At this point there were still paperback houses – Penguin, Pan, Panther, Arrow, New English Library – who were independent of the older, traditional hard-cover publishers. This was before the days of vertical integration. *Wrappings* sold out in its original hardback edition, and we did a paperback reprint.

Our first printer was Walter Stone at the Wentworth Press, a stalwart of the Fellowship of Australian Writers and editor of *Biblionews*. He was a familiar and generous and knowledgeable figure in that world of book-collectors and bibliographers and enthusiasts for Australian writing, the group that had sustained the preservation of the history of Australian literature before the universities offered any much recognition of it. His press published and printed *Southerly* and occasional literary bibliographies and historical books. But when we planned on producing a large format collection of Ron Cobb's cartoons, we found that Wentworth Press did not have the appropriate printing technology or available paper stock, so we moved to Roger Barnes at

Southwood Press. We then stayed with Southwood for all of our titles, and it was at that point that we decided to publish all our list directly into paperback.

Our decision to publish our first titles in hardback had ensured the books were reviewed. Paperbacks tended to get disregarded in the literary pages. But once our first titles had been noticed and well-reviewed, the literary editors were alerted to our existence, and our paperbacks were then reviewed.

The shift to initiate everything in paperback allowed for a lower retail price, which was important for our potential market. And it looked contemporary. The times they were a-changing. This was the age of disposable products. Already University of Queensland Press was publishing poetry and, from 1972, fiction directly into paperback; though they also issued a small hardback edition of the fiction, for library sales. Our Wentworth Press hardbacks looked somewhat old-fashioned. Retro, maybe, you could claim. Our new paperbacks had a contemporary look and feel that chimed in with the sense of cultural revival of those 'It's Time' times. It marked us off from the established, establishment publishers who persisted in first publishing in hardback; so you had to wait a year or so for a paperback, and not everything came out in paperback, either.

But our first book was something else again, and it appeared before the Viidikas and Adamson went into production. Jon Silkin, the English poet and editor of the literary magazine *Stand* was coming to Australia in 1974, attached to the University of Sydney as the first writer in residence in a newly established Literature Board scheme. Well, I had arranged that since I had known Jon for a while and he had appointed me Australian editor of *Stand*. It was an excellent magazine and I was able to publish a number of emerging Australian writers in it, getting them international exposure as we saw it – notably Bob Adamson's poems and the early stories of Vicki Viidikas and Peter Carey. Though my editorial role had its problems, since Jon and his wife Lorna Tracy had the final say. When they rejected material I had solicited, that put me in a difficult position and alienated a few fellow writers.

Jon had a new book coming out from a small press in England, Michael Schmidt's Carcanet Press, after Chatto & Windus had dropped him from their list. These were the years when literary publishers were first beginning to shed their poetry lists. Either Jon or I came up with the idea of an Australian edition to sell on the reading tour he planned. Jon was good at selling his books and magazine at readings – or anywhere else for that matter. He was once observed working the queue outside a London theatre. At some point he bumped into a busker working the queue from the other end, and sold the busker a copy of *Stand*.

So we arranged with Carcanet for our imprint to go on the title page and imported a swag of copies, another hardback. Leon Cantrell, a book collector and academic from the University of Queensland who was staying with me on a visit to Sydney, said it was the ugliest book he had ever seen and collapsed into mocking mirth on my couch. I considered throwing him and his wife Libby out onto the street but in the end simply went to bed in a huff. It certainly was not an attractive jacket, but it wasn't our design. Not our fault. We could have printed a new jacket, I suppose. When we published the Australian edition of Silkin's next book of poems from Carcanet, Pat in fact did just that. But that was later. In the meantime we promoted this one, *The Principle of Water*.

Rudi Krausmann invited us all up to Scotland Island to go sailing. The dinghy sank on the way to his yacht.

Silkin flailed desperately in Pittwater, calling out that he could not swim.

'What!' said Rudi in disgust, 'his book is called *The Principle of Water* and he cannot swim!'

'If Silkin drowns,' Pat said, 'it'll be great promotion for the book.'

An alumna of Hollywood High, she was adept at seeing publicity angles. But Silko (as Vicki always referred to him) was dragged safely ashore by his wife.

And then there was Cobb. Ron Cobb had drawn his unique cartoons for the *LA Free Press*. For a time Pat had lived in Los Angeles with Eric Matlen, who published Cobb's first two books, *RCD-25* and *Mah Fellow Americans*. Ron and Eric fell out after Eric broke his leg in a motorcycle accident, became increasingly paranoid from massive doses of cortisone and started dressing up in high heels and tights. Cobb had visited Australia, and returned to Los Angeles with an Australian wife, Robin Love, who had organised his tour for the National Union of Students. I found him an enigmatic character, quiet, withdrawn, modest about his achievements. He would chuckle gently, but never seemed the confrontational radical you might have imagined from his cartoons, many of them powerful indictments of the war in Vietnam. Cobb had served there, in the secret service. When we visited him in West Hollywood he was painting Nazi insignia on Word War II German helmets for a collector. Later he did a couple of monsters for *Star Wars* and the spaceship, uniform and symbols for *Alien*.

He agreed to Pat's proposal to publish a book of his cartoons. From the American collections of his work and from cartoons he had contributed to *The Digger* while in Australia, we made a selection. We left out most of the anti-war cartoons since the war was now over, the US defeated. Now those cartoons were dated, we wanted to move on, and we wanted the collection to look contemporary.

We did *The Cobb Book* as a large format paperback, 280 x 220 mm. It proved a great commercial success for us, and was often reprinted after its first edition in 1975. Bootlegged, too, by various overseas pirates. Soon we were assembling the cartoons we had omitted, all the anti-war ones, and searching around for others and in 1976 we made a second selection, *Cobb Again.* These two titles proved to be the financial underpinning of Wild & Woolley: the titles that made the money and kept us in business.

One time Pat and I drove to a book launch in my Falcon station wagon – Pat says it was to Canberra though I remember it as Melbourne. We put Cobb and co in the back seat, called in at Southwood Press in Marrickville, and loaded up Cobb books in the boot space in the back. The weight flattened out the suspension, and at every bump in the road there was a horrible grating noise. We turned back, unloaded a few boxes. But once in a while, all the way down to Canberra, the suspension made that funny noise. And ever after.

Cobb generously drew our logo for us. An imaginary animal, half American buffalo, half Australian kangaroo, to embody our origins.

The buffaroo. I think he thought I was Australian. I didn't demand a British lion. I was happy to be Australian.

Later he did a splendid cartoon of the buffaroo atop the Opera House, F-111's strafing at it, a contemporary King Kong. It said something about how embattled we were beginning to feel.

'Are you publishing your own novels?' someone asked me.

I wasn't. Vanity publishing was a terrible sneer in those days. Still is. An extraordinary illusion, as if commerce validated a book, and putting your money where your mouth is somehow discredited it. It is one of those labels that enable the idle to dismiss books without reading them, judging on the basis of an imprint.

Anyway, I wasn't planning on self-publishing now that University of Queensland Press had published my stories, *Aspects of the Dying Process*, in 1972 and was about to publish my first novel, *Living Together*.

'How can you expect writers to publish with Wild & Woolley if you don't publish your own books? It looks like you don't have any faith in the company.'

I forget who said that. Possibly Pat herself. It was a point. I hadn't thought of it, but I did now.

And I had a new novel, *The Short Story Embassy*, a novel quite unlike anything else I had done before, and quite unlike anything else in print in Australia – short, self-referential, post-modern before the term was current. I doubted that UQP would appreciate it.

Even as I had completed my previous novel, *Living Together*, I was worried about it. It was a consciously structured, patterned novel, the ghost of Henry James lurking there. I felt that the days of such novels were over. They weren't, of course, and it proved very popular. But at this point in the mid-70s I was committing myself to exploring a more open-ended, spontaneous form, to moving on from the aesthetic of Henry James into the spontaneity of Jack Kerouac, Leonard Cohen, Richard Brautigan. This was the agenda behind the stories we were publishing in the magazine *Tabloid Story*. *The Short Story Embassy* was a breakthrough for me. Yet, as Carl Harrison-Ford gleefully pointed out, the spirit of Henry James was still there; what was the title *The Short Story Embassy* but another formulation of James's 'The House of Fiction'?

Colin Talbot phoned from Melbourne. He said he was editor for a new press that Morry Schwartz, Fred Milgrom, Mark Gillespie and he were starting, Outback Press. Did I have a manuscript?

'I'm starting a press too,' I said.

I wondered, should I give *The Short Story Embassy* to an unknown, untested press from Melbourne?

'Don't give it to them,' said Pat, 'give it to us.'

Good thinking, Pat. Why give it to someone else when your own company was there looking for manuscripts? It was not even a matter of rivalry, just plain common sense. So should I give it to Wild & Woolley and risk the accusation of self-publishing? At least that way I could make sure the review copies all went off, at least I would have access to complimentary copies to give to friends and agents of influence.

In the end the issue of demonstrating confidence in our own press proved triumphant. We published *The Short Story Embassy* with Wild & Woolley in 1975 in paperback. And we published my next book, too, *Scenic Drive*, the following year, also in paperback. Because of its sexual preoccupations I did not even offer that one to UQP, I was sure the themes would prevent UQP from taking it. I had had to remove two stories from *Aspects of the Dying Process* when the University of Queensland vice-chancellor, Zelman Cowan, objected to them after Frank Thompson had shown him the manuscript. Queensland was an especially repressive state in those years. If there had been difficulties about my first book, there was no way *Scenic Drive* was going to be acceptable.

The war in Vietnam had ended but the habit of protest and direct action still rolled on. The women's movement was now a focus of energy and Pat became involved in a project that involved arranging publication support for Beryl Henderson's translation of a book about a French abortion trial, *Abortion: The Bobigny Affair*. It had an introduction by Simone de Beauvoir, whose book *The Second Sex* had been all the rage with the libertarians. Or at least with the female person libertarians.

Bobigny might seem remote from Australia, but no one in Australia had written anything equivalent. It was a similar situation to the anti-war movement when, back in 1966, I had been involved in publishing *Vietnam Briefing*, based on a debate in the Oxford Union. Again, the issue was immediately relevant but there was no Australian text on hand so we had reprinted this British pamphlet as a matter of urgency to get the debate moving.

'It's not the sort of book you really want to publish, is it?' said an editor from Collins who was wooing me in the way publishers were said to. He introduced me to Sir Billy Collins, but they never published me. Anyway, was *Abortion* the sort of book I wanted to publish? Why not? A literary list in tandem with a social issues list seemed the classic way to go. That was where we went. We designed a black and white cover with bold red lettering to signify the immediacy of a newspaper, black and white and read all over, as they used to say, and we published it in paperback. We met at the New Hellas restaurant overlooking Hyde Park with some of the people in the collective helping fund it. One of them, Edna Ryan, slipped as she left the raised platform of the window seat and broke her hip. We felt guilty for having arranged to meet there in that venue of libertarians and the *Bulletin*.

Pat had left her involvement with Tomato Press, but she brought along a little pamphlet, *All About Grass*, with which they had made some money when they published it in 1973. It told you how to grow your own marijuana. Well, growing your own marijuana was pretty simple. You just put a seed in some soil. Or in a pot of potting mix if you didn't have soil. Still, for those who had not been brought up to the pleasures and slavery of gardens in their childhood, this production told you such dubiously arcane information as which way to plant the seed (round end or sharp end down, recalling the debate about how to eat eggs in *Gulliver's Travels*) and, rather more usefully, how much earth with which to bury it (not a lot, just sprinkle a covering on top). And don't over water it. *All About Grass* was an alternative, counter-cultural text, originally written by Phil West, who had assigned copyright to Pat, and gradually added to by others. It was clearly American since it opened with a diatribe about the socialist evils of the state providing free medical care. I removed that bit, and added in a few literary anecdotes and odds and ends I had gleaned about grass in my reading, and in 1976 we reprinted it. It was a strangely shaped production, long and thin, not bound but stapled, and its cover the same cheap paper stock as the text. The Tomato Press production had had a coloured, stiffer cover. But we did this reprint cheaply. The aesthetics of the underground, we rationalised. Along with the Cobb books, it generated an ongoing profit stream that subsidised the literary titles. And established our credentials as alternative, anti-establishment, counter-cultural. All those buzz words.

Pat's basic and only significant income came from working for her friend Maureen Argy, who had a typesetting business, Composet. Maureen let Pat have access to the equipment after hours in exchange for cleaning her office. The office was down near Dixon Street in what is now Chinatown, but then had not been institutionalised and tourist-packaged as such. It was an area of fruit and vegetable warehouses, with Chinese restaurants on the floor above the warehouses, gambling joints behind and above them, cabbage leaves in the street, the markets round the corner. Pat sat there at night, typesetting our books. Jon Silkin gave an inaugural reading round the corner in the Teachers Federation. He complained that I did not attend. But I had heard him read before, many times. Best not to monopolise him, good to give other literary aspirants access. I had arranged the venue, given him his books to sell, and now I was occupied productively pasting in corrections to *The Short Story Embassy* while Pat typeset away, the portable television flickering in the corner of the room.

'I can't do this,' I said.

I was hopeless at such tasks, woodwork had been a nightmare at school, I was a writer, not a craftsman or a rude mechanical. Pat disregarded my diffidence and hopelessness. She had that American supreme self-confidence that anyone could do anything. Log cabin to White House. She showed me how to use the ruler, the knife, how to cut out the corrected line she had typeset, run rubber adhesive along the back of it, position it and stick it on top of the erroneous original. The adhesive stuck to the knife blade and I wiped it clean on the leg of my jeans, fraying the fabric in the course of time. And in the course of time I was able to line up the lines in a straight line. Once I was even given some typesetting to do, just a line or so. It was all an invaluable hands-on practicality, a change from living in my head, thinking purely literary thoughts. Not quite the craft activity of William Morris's Kelmscott Press or Jack Lindsay's Fanfrolico. A new technology for a new age. Gradually I lost that ingrained English defeatism, that resistance to doing anything different and difficult, that peasant suspicion of change and the new. It was time-consuming and tedious. But so was scholarly research. So was reading. So was gardening, for that matter. But it all served to reconnect me with the physical world, with soil and paper, blades and forks, watering cans and solvents.

One of the things it taught me about was the instability of the text. A useful scholarly reminder for my day job teaching literature at the university. Both Pat and I had a feeling for the look of the books, for the typography, the presentation. As a teenager I had pored over Oliver Simon's *An Introduction to Typography* and S. H. Steinberg's *Five Hundred Years of Printing*, a couple of treasured Pelicans from the days of Allen Lane's practical, visionary agenda.

After typesetting and pasting up the books, once in a while a story or a chapter would end with just a line or two carrying over to a page on its own. It looked strange. It was also uneconomical. I was always keen to economise, reduce the number of pages, save paper costs. A publisher's trait: André Deutsch was notorious for switching off electric lights in other peoples' houses, nothing personal, just a sense of economy.

'Fix that, Wild,' Pat instructed. And fix it I did, with a bit of re-paragraphing, even a bit of rewriting, deleting the odd word or two, so that the text contracted and there was no run-over.

That was when I discovered that Pat habitually rewrote the material she typeset.

'But you can't do that.'

'Why not? I always do,' she said. 'Most of them can't write. Or spell.'

She had always rewritten as she typeset for *Private Eye*, London *Oz*, whatever. Rewritten to fit in with the design, improve the sense, remove incomprehensibility.

'This is literature,' I protested.

'This?' she said, derisively. 'Literature? So what, anyway?' she might have added, and probably did.

'You can't just change things.'

'They never notice,' she said.

She was right about that.

I had never envisaged publishing as more than a part-time activity. I had my university job, I was writing fiction, editing *Tabloid Story*, editing the Asian and Pacific Writing series for UQP. Publishing was something to do amidst all the other activities that crowded in. It was a very different matter for Pat. She was doing some typesetting for her friend's business, but she needed other sources of income. Through the Collins connection I met Sonny Mehta, the legendary publisher who had set up Paladin, the quality imprint, when he was with Panther books, and had commissioned Germaine Greer's *The Female Eunuch*. He told me that when Pan lured him to join them, the sweetener was having his own quality list, Picador. He took me on a walk round the Sydney bookshops, checking out whether the Picador titles were on display.

'We only print 7000,' he told me, 'and the reps don't like having to bother with them.'

He impressed me with his hands-on approach, actually going into a bookshop. And with the modest print runs of quality paperbacks. From a Wild & Woolley perspective 7000 was a lot; but for an international paperback publisher, not many at all.

He had acquired a new title, *Rock Dreams,* paintings of rock stars. I remember Ray Charles in shades, driving a car. It was one of those titles destined to be a cult, or a commercial failure. He wanted it promoted. I suggested Pat for the job, she was from LA, after all, knew all about rock music. Wild & Woolley was not losing money, but nor was it making enough to support Pat. She got the job, and was able to use that experience to get hired by UQP for some further promotional work, and by the Australia Council's Literature Board to promote their expanded program of publishing support.

'There are some people calling themselves publishers who don't even have a warehouse,' declared Ken Wilder, the managing director of the local branch of William Collins, one of the English companies dominating the Australian publishing industry. We knew who he meant. He meant Pat and me.

There we were on Sunday morning educational television, out at the Channel 7 studio at 7 am, broadcasting live I seem to remember, but maybe just taping it in down-time. The program was called 'Television Tutorial' and was presumably designed to fill some sort of licensing requirements for the station, the provision of educational programming. But television was television, and when invited, we went. Publicity was the name of the game. Far more important than having a warehouse. Cheaper, anyway. Publishing was news, and our small press activities were attracting media attention.

True, we didn't have a warehouse. We stored the books beneath Pat's bed in Birchgrove. The bed was becoming higher and harder the more books we published and she complained bitterly. We tried shifting some of the stock from her place at Long Nose Point to mine in Wharf Road, carrying boxes up the flight of stairs to where I lived. She turned a worrying shade of green with the exertions and I could not bear to watch.

But soon we had our warehouse. Pat had decided she could not survive on hand to mouth contract work. I was all right, I had a full-time job. But Pat had no regular source of income other than the work she did typesetting and the occasional promotional contracts that came her way. So we went for the option of building up the business, making it make money. She took a mortgage on a house in Chippendale, which for a single woman was hard to do in those days. One bank manager insisted she get her father to sign the documents: she walked out.

The financial details, as ever, I shied away from. As Pat put it, 'You didn't have anything to do with the finance. It was all very much hand to mouth. Until the 80s, and after I sold the Chippendale place, there just wasn't any cash.' Pat's recollection is that we had each initially put $2000 into the company: 'We kept logs of how much time each put in. When the amount of time I had put in got to be about $4000 over Michael's, I wanted him to equal that with money. He didn't want to, so I took $4000 out of the company, Michael lent me, I think, $6000, and I used the $10,000 as a deposit, and bought the Chippendale tenement. It cost $23,000 in 1975. Esanda Finance lent me the rest on a ten year high interest loan, because I didn't "qualify" for their ANZ bank homeowners' one.' She calculates that during the period we worked together on Wild & Woolley, over five years her 'total gross income was $26000, or slightly over $5000 per year'.

The downstairs was the warehouse and office, Pat lived upstairs.

Office equipment was minimal. When the Sydney University English department acquired a new photocopier, they let me take the old one they were throwing out. At some point it caught fire. When Pat called for service, all sorts of alarms and hassles erupted: it was still registered as belonging to the university, and it was thought we had stolen it. Grand theft.

We expanded our distribution and began importing more books from the USA, stocking the entire City Lights list, and adding to it James Laughlin's New Directions, John Martin's Black Sparrow and Donald Allen's Four Seasons and Grey Fox Presses. Later we added some New York alternative presses: Dick Higgins' Something Else Press and Out of London Press, the Fiction Collective, Richard Kostelanetz and Henry Korn's Assembling Press, and Journeyman Press from the UK. For a while we also distributed Silkin's *Stand* magazine, but some young literary type persuaded Jon that we weren't doing a very good job and he could do better, and so Jon took it away from us and gave it to him. He didn't do better. We took on a couple of Sydney poetry presses, Bob Adamson's Prism Books and Phil Roberts' Island Press, and we reciprocally distributed Outback Press from Melbourne, they handling us down there for a while. The Outback titles included Kate Jennings' *Cry to Me My Melancholy Baby* and her anthology of women's verse, *Mother I'm Rooted*, Laurie Clancy's *A Collapsible Man*, Colin Talbot's *Massive Road Trauma*, *The Outback Reader*, edited by Michael Dugan and John Jenkins, and poems and plays by Garrie Hutchinson and Steven J. Spears. The *New Poetry* Prism poets included Robyn Ravlich, Tim Thorne, Dorothy Porter, Dorothy Hewett, Charles Buckmaster and Max Williams, while Island Press had Kevin Gilbert's *End of Dream-Time*, Martin Johnston's translations of modern Greek poetry, *Ithaka*, Adamson's *Swamp Riddles*, Phil's own collection *Crux*, and the annual *Poet's Choice* anthology. Other Australian presses we represented included Makar, Sisters, Rigmarole of the Hours, Adelaide University Union Press, Norstrilia and Horan, Wall and Walker.

Some titles sold well – like Allen Ginsberg's *Howl.* Most did more modestly. But by stocking the entire list of these presses, in limited numbers – 20, 50, 100 – we had a sufficient range of product to make the distribution programme financially viable. Postage costs were not as high as they are now. I think there was still a printed matter preferential rate. We had a handful of regular bookshops who ordered from us, and generally paid their bills on time. Although we supplied sale or return, there were rarely returns of this imported material – partly because the titles were never ordered in large numbers. These were the days when books were treated pretty much with respect, before they were dumped into large bins at the front of the shop and sold like vegetables on special.

So in the end we had a warehouse and I discovered its unique pleasures. Walls lined with books. All the treasures of the international *avant-garde*. It was an esoteric list. I walked along the shelves picking

up a sample copy here, another there. My library swelled as I added the new arrivals week by week, supplementing the second-hand books, remainders and review copies I had collected. Of course, there is no such thing as a free book. When the partnership was dissolved I was billed for the cost of them. Even at trade discounts it was quite a bill.

At one point the university registrar phoned up my Head of Department to inquire about my commercial activities. The university in the 70s was still properly committed to university values: it had not yet rushed headlong into the embrace of commerce. No more had I. Wild & Woolley's commercial activities, what a joke.

The head of department, Leslie Rogers, was suitably uncooperative. Professors at that time resented administrators interfering in departmental affairs. Leslie had edited *Isis*, too, and for a while had been a journalist on the Glasgow *Daily Record*. He was a specialist in Old English and never showed much interest in the sort of contemporary writing I was promoting. He had done war service in India and had no sympathy with my anti-Vietnam war activities; indeed, he would go round the department corridors, ripping down notices of anti-war readings that I had posted up. But he defended me from the administrators, for which I was grateful.

I could argue, and I did, that these publishing and distribution activities were an adjunct to my other literary activities – lecturing to students, writing critical essays for academic journals, book reviewing. Distribution provided an income stream and sufficient product to allow us to hire a rep. But the material was not simply there to make money. It was there because we believed in it. This was quality literature, *avant-garde* literature, the experimental. What we were doing had its cultural, educational mission. It was important that this material should be available in Australia.

The year before setting up the press I had been visiting Jon Silkin in Newcastle-upon-Tyne and had called in at a bookshop in which he was briefly a partner. It was one of Jon's schemes on the theme of how a poet might make a living, and it was not a success. The business partner turned out to be somewhat dodgy. When he disappeared, or went to gaol, he left Jon's wife Lorna his mescaline cactus, whether as an outright gift, or to tend until he returned, I cannot remember. This was not Jon's scene at all – though oddly an early *Stand* had published Ginsberg's poem on LSD. Anyway, amongst the stock I discovered a new City Lights book, Charles Bukowski's *Erections, Ejaculations and Other Tales of Ordinary Madness*. I bought it, read it, and was much taken by it. This would sell in Sydney, I thought, but this was before I had met Pat. It stuck in my mind, and was one of the reasons, apart from my earlier enthusiasm for the Beats, Kerouac particularly, that inspired our decision to distribute City Lights titles.

Lawrence Ferlinghetti, who had set up City Lights, was an anarchist, which can be progressive – as in William Lane's positive assessment of anarchists in *The Workingman's Paradise* – or reactionary, as with many of the members of the Sydney Libertarians. But anarchism allows progressive elements to flourish. And Ferlinghetti was the publisher of choice for the Beats – Ginsberg, Kerouac, Diane di Prima, and so on.

Ferlinghetti's own poetry was published by James Laughlin's New Directions press, along with Gary Snyder and Gregory Corso. Apart from the Beats, Laughlin's list had something of a right wing agenda: Ezra Pound, Nabokov, Céline, and so on. But there was also William Carlos Williams's poems, Kenneth Rexroth's translations from the Japanese, et cetera. And there was the exciting annual anthology of new writing, *New Directions*, which always contained cutting edge material. Whatever the political motivation that may have lain behind it in those Cold War years, New Directions was without doubt a quality list. It was the writing that appealed to me at that time; the politics worried me more later.

And then there was John Martin's Black Sparrow list. Martin had been a collector of D. H. Lawrence, and told us he had founded his press by selling off a Lawrence manuscript. Lawrence, too, can be seen as a right wing writer – though in my *Political Fictions* I tried to recuperate him for the left. And Wyndham Lewis, whom Martin began extensively to reprint, certainly had some extreme right wing leanings. But he was a great writer. So was Paul Bowles, also reprinted by Black Sparrow.

And it was Black Sparrow that had continued to publish Bukowski. The problem was though, John Martin told us, that Bukowski would go on reading tours around the university campuses, and his student fans would try and get him drunk.

'Anyone can get Bukowski drunk,' he complained. 'It's not difficult. It's easy. And one day they're going to kill him.'

And since Bukowski was his best-selling author, pretty well the financial engine of his entire list, he found the prospect worrying.

We made all these books available. Not just a few lead titles but the entire lists, except for those titles unavailable because of copyright restrictions. Most of it had been unavailable in Australia before.

It has been remarked more than once how Donald Allen's Grove Press anthology *The New American Poetry* had such a profound influence on the Australian poets of the late 1960s and the 1970s. We distributed Allen's own presses, Four Seasons and Grey Fox, and we met Allen in Bolinas. He had just received a good review for one of his titles in the *New York Times* and was delighted. I was surprised how much it meant to him. To me he was a major literary figure, a fountainhead. But in the USA he was clearly marginal to the New York commercial publishing and reviewing establishment. We visited the poet and playwright Michael McClure in San Francisco. He had broken through into the East Coast with a novel from a mainstream publisher. It had not been a success. 'They treat novels like gambling chips,' he said. 'They grab a handful, put them out on the market and see which ones come up.'

This was all both depressing, and cheering, as we carried on in our own marginalisation.

But our project was to bring the margins to the centre and for a while we succeeded. We got these important books around. It was a major intervention into the cultural map of the nation. We represented literary movements only touched upon by mainstream publishing. Nabokov and Kerouac had occasionally got around. But by bringing in these lists we comprehensively represented the best of the available American *avant-garde* – plus a fair bit of the European. Later Pat took on John Calder's UK list which had a strong European *avant-garde* cultural cohesion, Beckett, the *nouveau roman* and so on.

Not all of the writers we imported I totally admired. I was out of sympathy with the reactionary politics of many of them. But their formal explorations, their creative vision, were impressive. It would have been nice if there had been some good *avant-garde* presses with a left wing agenda that we could have represented too. But insofar as there were any left wing presses, they had little interest in literature, confining themselves to politics and in due course theory, with an occasional foray into some proletarian aesthetic. I had written positively about Lawrence and Sillitoe's proletarianism; but I didn't see proletarianism as a desirable way of life or an appealing aesthetic. I had lived that. Not much fun. Kerouac had lived it too, and had chosen to grow beyond it.

Years later I donated my entire personal library to the University of Western Sydney. For a tax advantage. Nothing wrong with philanthropy if you can get a tax advantage. Bob Adamson tells me that once in a while a young poet from UWS visits him and discusses in detail the work of some West Coast American poet he has discovered.

'How did you find him?' Bob asks.

'In the library,' is the answer.

So that collection continues to have its uses. And I made sure most of the material we represented was ordered for Fisher Library at the University of Sydney, too. Recondite texts, alternative analyses, seminal influences, all that richness of a literary tradition that so easily passes by academia unnoticed. Now it is there. Unless they decide to purge it.

Bookshops can be a delight, but warehouses are something else again. They contain all sorts of amazing titles never seen in the shops: something we found out to our cost. But, for a while, it seemed worth it.

These were the heady years of the small press boom, when independent presses sprang up and thrived, in the USA, in Australia and, a bit more belatedly, in Britain. In California there was that mythic organisation called Book People that handled distribution for the myriad of alternative publishers. They issued bulky, illustrated catalogues which occasionally reached Australian shores, and the poets and book freaks pored over them with all the salivatory excitement supposed to be the preserve of the readers of *Playboy* and *Penthouse*. When we got to San Francisco, Book People was where we went. It was like the treasure cave in *The Count of Monte Cristo*. It was one of those dawns in which it was bliss to be alive. Even when the bill came in, it was worth it.

Warehouses are at the very heart of the book trade. They are far more central than mere editorial offices. Much of the editing is contracted out now, anyway. But warehouses remain the publisher's pride and joy. When ten years later I first published with Penguin, I was taken on an initiatory tour of their warehouse. Scratch any publisher and he or she will wax lyrical about their warehouse. Even those who no longer publish lyric poems. It is the same at the retail end. The mystique of on-line bookselling has done wonders for Amazon dot com's contemporary high-tech image, but it is only the ordering that is done through cyber space. The books still have to be stored in a vast warehouse somewhere up near Seattle.

'You've got to remember,' Minas Poulos, who became our book trade rep, once told me, 'publishing is all about the logistics of forklift trucks.'

I remember seeing Lawrence Ferlinghetti striding down the streets of San Francisco. And what was he doing? Declaiming one of his poems? Composing one? Signing autographs? No, he was carrying boxes of books into the City Lights warehouse. It cheered me up in the years

ahead as I shifted boxes of books from shelf to shelf back in Australia. The literary life, with all its heavy lifting.

For most readers and writers and book collectors, books are objects to be treasured, valued, hoarded. But professionals in the book trade soon get blasé. Damaged copies get tossed unceremoniously into the garbage. Visiting Angus & Robertson's publishing headquarters one time I found out on the pavement a rubbish bin with thrown out copies of a book on defence policy in South-East Asia. It was not an area I knew much about, but I eagerly retrieved a copy. I never read it. But it gave another recondite note to my library. I looked at it affectionately as I passed it day by day. It was like saving a stray dog from the pound.

The garbage bin was one of the first places I looked whenever I walked into the Wild & Woolley warehouse. There was usually some slightly scuffed or creased copy there: a slim paperback of Jack Kerouac's poems, or a handbook on marijuana by Winona Ryder's dad, crushed in its travels through the mail. I would carefully salvage it. One day I noticed the entire staff, all two of them, were sitting laughing at me. Knowing my obsession, they had been deliberately putting books into the garbage bin when they heard me arrive. No doubt they billed me for the copies I retrieved.

There was one warehouse I remember going to where the books were free, Tudor distributors. It was in the years when English Literature was a huge and, it seemed, an endlessly expanding educational subject. It attracted large numbers of students, and publishers were making vast profits on publishing books that were used as texts, many of them out of copyright. Consequently they were generous in giving out free inspection copies to teachers and academics. One free copy might result in the book being prescribed as a set text with orders for anything from fifty to a thousand copies. I remember collecting a marvellous stack of Mark Twain, Herman Melville, Thoreau and Henry James in those elegant Signet Classics editions, which I treasured for years. I even set some of them as texts on my courses.

Now English studies have shrunk and collapsed, the small presses have shrivelled away, but there are still a few distributors who let you roam through their warehouses and share their delight in the romance of the forklift truck.

Though it was a while before Pat got her forklift. At this stage everything was done by hand. Any hands we could conscript. My five-year-old daughter Sunny was put to work, using our old rubber-stamp to stamp the return address on the packets of books we sent out. She tells me, 'I still have fond memories of rubber stamping, receiving my $5 and then someone (Don'o Kim?) trying to give me $10 to replace the $5 and being extremely wary of this suspicious transaction.' Wrapping and dispatching was a basic skill. The absolutely basic skill, according to Dennis Wren, who had come out from England to run Heinemann's local branch, and then set up Wren books. He had learned how to tie knots and wrap parcels back in East Anglia as a fifteen-year-old with W. H. Smith's wholesale newspaper and book business. Wrapping parcels and having lunch, that was the publishing life, Dennis assured me.

We spent hours rearranging our warehouse. A new shipment of books would arrive through the mail, and the shelves would become too crowded for the new stock. We would make space, move the books from one press to another position, then move the books from another press somewhere else again. We would buy new shelving. On it went. Hours. I told myself it was valuable physical exercise.

For the first time the full range of City Lights and New Directions books was available in Australia, all those books from the Beats and the associated American *avant-garde*, and there was a demand for it. It had been scarce, hard to obtain, but at the same time people knew of its existence. We were not having to market the totally new and untested. The books we brought in had been heard of and were wanted. Similarly with the Australian writing. The writers we published with Wild & Woolley were not totally unknown. Most of them – Robert Adamson, Vicki Viidikas, myself, Kris Hemensley, Laurie Duggan, Colin Talbot, Denis Altman, David Foster, Christine Talbot – had already published one or two books. We had all broken through the first barriers and had got into print, had a reputation as 'new' writers; it was a small step, but it made the task of getting the books into the shops easier. Known but not well-known. Emergent. The beginnings of a movement.

For all its being an emerging movement, we had no manifesto. Our publishing policy evolved as we went along. But we did make one initial resolution: we would not publish poetry.

This might be the appropriate occasion to make my position on poets clear. I am not against them. In fact, I think they are a rather good idea. Both poets and poetry. And you can't have one without the other. So we are stuck with poets. I have written about them in the past, not always in flattering terms. But that is the problem when you write fiction; or memoir; you can't always be flattering about other people. Especially poets.

The thing about poets is that they have, they emanate, this energy, this force field of disorder and disruption and desire, they are like Pan. What is he doing, the great God Pan, down in the reeds by the river? Well, what he's doing is luring you with the poetry he pipes, luring you to your destruction, or at least incapacitation, ignominy, dismissal, divorce or despair. Freedom, too. But at a price. Poets are like Boudu, the tramp in Jean Renoir's film *Boudu Saved from Drowning*; the bourgeois couple save his life and he rewards them by utterly subverting theirs.

And that is the point of poets and poetry of course. It should be the point of all writers, subverting the way we've been habituated to see the world. But more and more the novelists are being subverted by the entertainment industry and the glamour of large advances and three-book contracts, so they carefully avoid saying anything subversive. They have become, or want to become, like celebrities: and celebrities, like politicians, can't afford to say anything. They have to follow the rule of the old Irish proverb, whatever you say, say nothing. Well, it's sad that novelists have gone that way. Maybe some of the poets have even tried. But basically no one has yet seen a way regularly to squeeze big money out of poetry. So the poets remain in their pristine, original, disturbing, disruptive purity. In that respect, anyway.

I have always valued my acquaintance with poets, disturbing though many inevitably were. I got some good stories out of them, anyway. Always grateful for anything that produces a good story. But there's more to writing than the story. And it's the way poets are preoccupied with language, with image, with making you read more slowly and with making you focus on the medium, language, and the riches it can offer, that I find so valuable. They bring language alive, they create it as they create with it, extending it, playing with it, probing out insights and truths with it. In the Renaissance it was the magical power of numbers that appealed to mathematicians, not our contemporary preoccupation with calculating interest and devising complex financial derivatives. There used then to be another mathematics, something separate from the concerns of the money men. And so with poetry, it provides access to another language. There still is another verbal language, with its mysterious and complex and magical powers, and the poets preserve it, and keep it distinct from the formulaic one-liners and situations of the entertainment industry. It is something richer and rarer and far more rewarding than the verbally transparent advertising copywriter's prose that is colonising fiction. The poets offer a last bastion of defence, preserving language as a medium, rather than as a necessary and perfunctory instrument.

Apart from Angus & Robertson and University of Queensland Press who were still publishing poetry, there were already a number of small press poetry publishers. Notably, Robert Adamson was running Prism poets, an offshoot of his magazine *New Poetry*; and Phillip Roberts was running Island Press, with its annual *Poet's Choice* anthology as well as individual new titles. Having taken on the distribution of both these lists, we had no wish to enter into competition with them in publishing poetry ourselves.

Phil had named his press after Scotland Island in Pittwater, where he had bought a block of land. He never built on the block, and ultimately sold it, moving to Bundeena south of Sydney, after living in Lavender Bay for a while. But Scotland Island maintained its literary connections, Rudi Krausmann living there for many years and producing his *avant-garde* magazine *Aspect – Art and Literature* there; and after that I moved there myself. So did Dennis and Dee Wren. But that was way in the future.

Phil had bought a hand press, and was conscientiously, if laboriously, hand-setting and hand-printing *Poet's Choice*. It was a labour of love, but it was still hard labour. One day he came over to Chippendale from the university, where he was a colleague of mine in the English Department, and saw Pat at work on the IBM composer. It was a revelation. He was so impressed by the comparative ease of it that he promptly gave up hand-setting and entered the modern age.

For all our decision not to publish poetry, nonetheless, ironically, our first book had been Jon Silkin's poems. And we had included some of Adamson's poems in *Zimmer's Essay*, some reprinted from his first book, some selected in advance from his next book, *Swamp Riddles*, which Island Press was publishing.

And then there was Nigel Roberts, who was a sort of fixture around Balmain and Rozelle. The Balmain scene was very much at the core of our original project. Bob Adamson, Vicki Viidikas, David Foster, Pat and I at various times lived there. Nigel was an early resident, and lives there still. He had produced an early alternative underground magazine *Free Poetry* with stencils and duplicator, and kept a sort of open house for poets, both local and visiting from interstate, where you would often be likely to find Bill Beard, Terry Gillmore, Johnny Goodall, Robert Harris, Shelton Lea, Pi O, Eric Beach, Kerry Leves, Tim Thorne and such like. All the bad boys looking for the good times. He had also been active in the Balmain readings, at which the literary folk, pub crowd, and not so beautiful people of the peninsula would gather on the waterfront and get drunk and stoned and hear each other deliver their latest compositions. Sometimes hurling emptied beer cans at readers they did not appreciate. I approached him for a manuscript and he gave us *In Casablanca For the Waters*.

He had a painting David Forbes had done of him that he wanted on his cover as a wrap-around. Wrap-arounds rarely work. Not when they are based on original art, rather than designed specifically as a cover. It was an unprepossessing sepia. But he wanted it. He was there, portrayed in it.

'Let him have it,' said Pat, sick of it, after delivery of the manuscript had dragged on for two or three years, Nigel one of those writers in virginal recoil from risking a first book.

'It's not going to sell, anyway,' she said.

From our distribution activities we knew that poetry didn't sell. Not well. We were figuring on printing a thousand copies minimum of our titles, and selling most of them, in order to survive, to avoid losing money. We could do that with fiction and essays. But poetry, we were to discover, was something that obstinately stuck at around two hundred copies.

Pi O, the Melbourne poet, a powerful performer, had mainly self-published his works before we took him on. He apologised that we moved only a couple of hundred of his *Pi O Revisited*. He had expected more. So had we.

We were equally unsuccessful with Didier Coste. He had been fêted in Paris for his first novel and was now teaching French at Sydney University. In the spirit of internationalism and *l'avant-garde sans frontières*, I asked him for a book. Somehow when *Vita Australis* was printed it came out the wrong size, the printer having omitted to follow Pat's instructions to enlarge the typesetting, which had been done at

70 per cent of the intended size. For some reason. But Didier was less concerned about that – we may not even have told him – than with the blurb's attribution of some important French prize to him which he hadn't won. Somewhere along we had got the name of the prize that he had won confused with this more distinguished one. But nobody else noticed. We were not into prizes. Adamson used to quote William Blake: 'There is no competition in heaven.'

Although we were making no money on poetry, somehow we continued to do it. Vicki Viidikas presented us with a manuscript of poems. We had done well with her stories, *Wrappings*. Was it sensible to refuse a book from one of our iconic authors? So in 1978 we published her *Knabel*. And then Laurie Duggan had been employed by Pat to help out in the warehouse, packing books. Wouldn't it be ridiculous not to publish the work of an engaging and well-respected poet who was working for the press? And he was in the Beat tradition – Philip Whalen, whose books we distributed, being a major influence on him at that time. And after all, the Beats had been a literary movement embracing poetry and prose: wasn't our new writing – no one ever came up with any other generic name for it – similar in that regard? So in 1978 we did his *Under the Weather*. And then there was Lee Cataldi, who had been a graduate student at Sydney University when I arrived there, Lee Sonnino in those days. I had sat as an invigilator in the Muniment Room beneath the clock tower when she and Germaine Greer had taken their entrance exams for Oxford and Cambridge. My first official task. After Oxford she had compiled *A Handbook of Renaissance Rhetoric* for Routledge & Kegan Paul, lectured at the University of Bristol, and then returned to Sydney where she was teaching at Tempe High School. I had re-encountered her at a series of seminars on politics and literature that Stephen Knight and I were putting on in the early evening in the English Department. She offered us a collection of poems, *Invitation to a Marxist Lesbian Party*. A first collection of poems was against all our instincts. But it was one of those books capturing the mood of those times. We published it in 1978. It was very successful, and won the Fellowship of Australian Writers Anne Elder award. She featured in due course on the NSW Higher School Certificate syllabus.

Maybe I argued for Billy Jones's manuscript *My Unshackled Hands* on the grounds that since he hand wrote and illustrated it in an artwork way – and it was beautifully done – we would save money by not having to typeset it. Well, save time, since the typesetting was still mainly done by Pat. When the book was published he gave me a framed drawing of a joint of marijuana, vibrating like a Van Gogh, just the sort of thing you needed on your wall.

And then Jill Jolliffe came in with some poems from the Timor independence movement by Francesco da Costa which she was going to self-publish, or publish through some organisation. I thought she was a friend of Pat's, Pat thought she was a friend of mine. We both thought collaboration with her might save in work and time and costs. It didn't. But we did the book.

I also offered to publish a collection of John Tranter's poems. Jon Silkin, who was there with me when we visited Tranter, was appalled. 'But you haven't even seen the manuscript,' he said. I never did. It never came.

None of the Australian poets had Jon Silkin's persistence and energy. Jon took a suitcase of books to every reading, made sure he sold copies, arranged a reading and selling tour to the United States every year, on top of his endless appearances round the British Isles. And Allen Ginsberg's *Howl* from City Lights just kept on selling.

Bob Adamson was one of the few to do well. But Bob was never worried about sales. He kept no precise reckoning. His practice was to give away copies of his books, or hand them out for review, because he published them himself and so could afford to. Bob and I both agreed on this strategy of splashing copies around, because that was the best and cheapest advertising. Still is. You can afford to give away a lot of copies for the price of a display advertisement in one of the weekend broadsheets. The point is to get copies to people so they can read them. That way the word spreads. Particularly if you target who you give them to. Agents of influence, as they call them in that other gentleman's profession. That was the advantage of being a publisher. To be able to give away books to people who might appreciate them. Indeed, that was the point of being a publisher as far as Bob and I could see it. And that way sales might take off. It was a theory, indeed a practice, that we followed, anyway. Though there were those in the trade who did not agree with us. But as for selling the books, that was something else again. We were not concerned with making guaranteed returns for shareholders. Bob would turn up at the Forth & Clyde with, hanging from his shoulder, his multi-coloured, tasselled Greek bag full of poems and pills and scrap-books and letters and copies of the latest *New Poetry* and copies of books, books he had published and books he had written. And he would dispense them. The idea at some point had no doubt been to sell copies of the magazine and the books down the pub, maybe at a discount, a special price for a tried and trusted friend, an old mate, anyone. Barter them, maybe, for a smoke or a drink or peanuts. But he usually ended up giving them away. Not indiscriminately. But to those writers and reviewers and artists and dealers and journalists and film-makers and aspiring politicians who turned up at the Newcastle and the Forth & Clyde and the Dry Dock and the William Wallace and the London and the art galleries and the readings and the Balmain barbecues. That was how the magazine became known and his books read. That was what helped him become a legend. 'Publishing,' Bob said to me, 'publishing is subterfuge.'

Pat had a particular interest in comics. As she told the vice-chancellor of the University of Sydney, Sir Bruce Williams, one time we were at the

Adelaide Writers' Festival, she had got through English at Hollywood High by reading *Classics Illustrated* comics. He was most interested. I stood there transfixed and tried to smile benignly. Thank you, partner.

Cobb's two books were making us money. Pat dug out her prized collection of rare underground comix from Melbourne, where she had lived for a while previously. There wasn't a lot of material, unlike the USA, but nonetheless it was a movement. A potential cult.

I suggested adding some Sydney material, and found some from the Libertarian's underground paper *Thorunka,* a Dave Bromley page from the Sydney University student paper *Honi Soit*, and copies of the original Sydney *Oz* magazine with some work by Martin Sharp. It was a somewhat earlier movement, but Sharp had later mutated to the next phase with the Mick Jagger image he created, so we included him. Important to have an historical sense about these things, I told Pat.

And so she edited *The Wild & Woolley Comix Book*. It was a successful collection, the first – and only – above ground representation of a breakthrough underground art. Occasionally we received angry letters from parents who had unwittingly bought the title for their children and found it full of drugs and sex. Lucky kids. We had letters of complaint about *All About Grass*, too.

Carl Harrison-Ford took a sanitised version of the idea with him to Cassells, where he was briefly employed. His father had been a commercial artist, and Carl was familiar with the Australian comics of the above ground, commercial variety. Cassells produced a substantial anthology of them – *Panel by Panel* by John Ryan.

Carl Harrison-Ford was helping us out running the warehouse and packing books. Like Leon Cantrell and Walter Stone and Roger Barnes and Kris Hemensley and Robert Adamson and myself, he was a great book collector. He had been involved with Adamson and others in the coup that seized control from Roland Robinson of *Poetry Magazine*, later renamed *New Poetry* to distinguish it more clearly from Grace Perry's earlier breakaway magazine *Poetry Australia*. Now, having lost his research scholarship in the English department, never having quite got round to putting enough if anything of his projected thesis down onto paper, he was reviewing books for the broadsheets and working for Sydney University Press as a proof-reader and packer. Some said he lived there, with a sleeping-bag, or was it a camp bed, hidden amidst the boxes of books in the packing room. I would have lunch with him and Malcolm Titt, the current manager, and the designer David New in the university staff club.

'Cash flow,' Malcolm would say ominously.

I nodded wisely. I had no idea what he meant but he seemed to think it would be our nemesis. Or its lack would be.

'And they'll regret the name, too,' he assured Carl.

That was one thing we never did regret.

As for cash flow, finances, all those sort of things, I can't say I ever really thought about them. Making money had never been a preoccupation. I had a good job, anyway. Academics were then comparatively well paid. I did not own a house, I was able to save, I had money in the bank. I didn't even remember how much I put into the company to start up. A thousand dollars? Two? I seem not to have kept any records.

In between dreaming up the press and getting started, the Australia Council had been created and absorbed the old Commonwealth Literary Fund. Money was allocated for publishing support. This had not been in our minds when we began. Indeed I was suspicious of government subsidies. They meant control, they encouraged you into a position of dependency. To see government involvement in the creative arts as hands-off, no-strings-attached altruism is naïve.

But when subsidies are in place, it is hard, if not impossible, to compete against the subsidised product without a subsidy yourself. We succumbed. We applied for funding. To our amazement, we received it. Over nine years we received subsidies for 27 of our titles. This was two-thirds of our list for the period that I was involved. Since our list was primarily literary, it was appropriate that we received Literature Board support for those titles. The other third consisted primarily of the cartoon, comix and dope books: the ones that made the money.

The Literature Board subsidies generally more or less covered our immediate printing costs. If we didn't cost our time and labour, we could get by. But that uncosted time and labour were required for editing, copy-editing, typesetting, formatting, design, pasting-up, proof-reading, promotion, publicity, marketing, advertising, and all the dealing with authors, printers, media and bookshops, let alone grant applications and acquittals. That was a lot of labour and time; but that was how Wild & Woolley survived. It was not a commercial proposition. Any significant surplus generated came from the non-literary list and the import and distribution side of the business. Even that was not lucrative. Minas Poulos, our trade rep, was paid a commission on sales. That was how we lost him to UQP when they made him an offer he could not refuse: a salary.

We received a flat subsidy for *Wrappings* and *Zimmer's Essay* and Kris Hemensley's collection of stories *Here We Are*. Then the Literature Board changed the way it calculated the subsidy, introducing some complex formulae. This was when the Literature Board first began losing its way, moving from subsidising the worthy but not commercial, to becoming a book support program for the industry. There was now a basic subsidy for a thousand copies, and then a variable additional amount depending on how many copies you printed, the amount of square centimetres of a book's page times the number of pages reduced by some other factor. Pat Healy, the Literature Board publications officer, told us to buy a calculator – until then we had been doing the sums by long division. We did, and worked out that if we printed 5000 copies of Antigone Kefala's *The First Journey* and 5500 of Rudi Krausmann's *From Another Shore,* the books would cost us no cash outlay.

Rudi's book, a collection of prose poems, had been rejected when we applied for a poetry subsidy. So we put it through again as fiction, and got support. Or was it the other way round? I forget that, too. One of those arbitrary decisions of the Board, presumably trying to boost fiction production.

We would have been irresponsible as publishers, I declared, formulating our response should it be required, if we had not done what was best for our authors.

It felt pretty irresponsible publishing 5000 copies of minority interest titles. But we did it. Economic necessity. However, after we had received and spent the money I made a point of telling someone on the Board, maybe the Director, Michael Costigan, and they changed the formula after that. Maybe it was when I was appointed to the Board, and felt I had better come clean.

Thirty years later Rudi and Antigone both gratefully took delivery of a couple of boxes of their books that Nicholas Pounder discovered in a store room at the university when he was looking for back issues of *Tabloid Story.* We never pulped them. We kept everything.

We even kept overruns of covers. We used to get the printer to trim them down to postcard size. Then we used them for 'with compliments' slips, brief correspondence, mail art exhibitions, and even for rejection slips. Rudi complained bitterly when we used the back cover art of his book, a full length photograph of him holding forth at a reading, to inform authors we were not accepting their manuscripts. The unhappy authors identified him with their rejection and blamed him for the decision.

New fiction was my first interest and the list I was most keen to develop. I had approached Kris Hemensley, a prolific small press author, and he offered us his collection of stories, *Here We Are*. Antigone Kefala sent us *The First Journey* which, like Vicki Viidikas' *Wrappings*, was her first fiction volume. A couple of authors who had published their first books with Macmillan came across to us, Christine Townend and David Foster. Christine Townend, who gave us her second book, *Travels with Myself*, was a gifted writer, but she didn't stay with fiction. She moved into animal rights, with *In Defence of Living Things*, *Voice for the Animals* and *Pulling the Wool*, and then in due course took off for an ashram in India. David Foster gave us a novel he had written in collaboration with a scientific colleague, D. K. Lyall, *The Empathy Experiment*, a weird and disturbing fantasy that may well have been true, about researches into drugs and psychic spying. I notice that he does not feature it in those 'by the same author' lists placed opposite the title pages of his recent books. We were not trying to poach. Rather, we were positioning ourselves as the publisher of choice for titles the big commercial houses shied away from. And in that context, we looked out for first novels, publishing one that the Literature Board refused to support, Chris Aulich's *It*, and another by Amitava Ray, *Baby Tiger*. The Salami Sisters sent a postcard with an offer, a manuscript, maybe, or perhaps just their fair selves for a visit. We invited them to come round, but they didn't. Pat says they did, but I was busy packing books and what they wanted was an editor to help them develop a manuscript. They were about to visit Melbourne, so we told them to visit McPhee Gribble. A pity, since their novel *Puberty Blues* did well and Kathy Lette has since gone stellar.

Dal Stivens sent us a manuscript. I made a tight selection from it – another one of our slim volumes – which focused on the quirky and innovative and experimental aspect of his fiction, and it was published as *The Unicorn and Other Stories* in 1977. Dal was a true original. 'It's always difficult to get published if you keep on doing something new,' he told me. He had been a prime mover with Walter Stone and Morris West in setting up the Australian Society of Authors. His first book, *The Tramp and Other Stories*, published back in 1938, had been praised by H. E. Bates and Graham Greene. For more than forty years he had continued to turn out a marvellous stream of realistic observation, tall stories, comic satires, fables, fantasies and visions. 'The Man Who Bowled Victor Trumper' stands as one of the jewelled touchstones of the Australian story, a fine example of the exploitation of excess, of which Stivens was a marvellous exponent. Later Outback Press made a selection of his cricket stories, *The Demon Bowler*. Slightly built and a habitual smoker, Dal had huge resources of energy. In an occupation not renowned for its taciturnity, he was a prodigious conversationalist. A phone call from Dal could fill your morning. And often did. I remember visiting him when we were establishing *Tabloid Story*, to which he was an early contributor. He was always helpful to other writers, young or old, and he was immensely helpful to us and full of support. When we rose thinking it was time to leave, he stood himself against his door, arms outstretched, to prevent the evening from coming to an end.

Morris Lurie sent us a collection, too. I think if he had sent it eighteen months later I would have published it. But when he sent it, right at the beginning, I was narrowly committed to a particular experimental, innovative, new writing, together with a confessional Beat aesthetic. Writing compatible with the City Lights program, rather than with New Directions' more traditional list. As we went on, I opened up the range of what we published. Partly because there wasn't that much confessional or experimental fiction around, and partly because we discovered that there was quality material in other modes that wasn't getting published. But at the time we told him he would probably do better with Outback in Melbourne since that was his home town: we would be distributing him in Sydney, anyway, if Outback took him. Which they did. And he went on to publish a number of titles

Tabloid Story
TABLOID STORY
Tabloid Story
Tabloid Story
Tabloid Story

with them. Not publishing Lurie was a decision I later regretted. Over the years I continued to read him, and was increasingly taken by the wit and economy and human observation of his writing.

We also began developing a substantial non-fiction list, something we had not initially envisaged. We asked Colin Talbot if he was interested in collecting his articles on what was loosely called popular culture – rock 'n' roll, festivals, lifestyle. Colin, apart from being a shaping editorial spirit of Outback Press, was also the *Australian*'s rock music correspondent; and had written some sustained pieces for those quasi-commercial, quasi-alternative papers that were around at the time – *Nation Review*, *The Living Daylights*, *The Digger* and others I no longer remember. We published it as *Colin Talbot's Greatest Hits* in 1977. We asked Albie Thoms, an experimental film-maker whom I had known from the Push, and who worked on *Skippy the Bush Kangaroo*, the television series, for his essays on *avant-garde* and alternative movies and the computerised future, and published them in 1979, a substantial collection, under the title *Polemics for a New Cinema*. And we asked Denis Altman, whom I knew from the university, for a collection of his occasional articles. His *Homosexual: Oppression and Liberation* had been a landmark book in the emergent gay movement, and I figured that his essays might have a significant market. We published them in hardback as *Coming Out in the Seventies*. I felt it was about as commercial as we wanted to go.

Penguin picked it up as a reprint from us: about as uncommercially up-market as they wanted to go, they said. It did well for both of us. Alyson in New York published an American edition with the Australian material cut out.

And then I approached Jack Lindsay. Nancy Keesing in a book review in the *Sydney Morning Herald* had remarked that someone should collect Jack's essays on Australian Literature. Since she was at that time chair of the Literature Board, this seemed a hint that we might be able to get a subsidy for such a collection, and we did. But the book grew substantially larger than a collection of Jack's Australian essays. He proposed including a whole range of pieces he had written on modern writing, not simply the Australian material, and it finally appeared as *Decay and Renewal: Critical Essays on Twentieth Century Writing* in 1976. It was a big project and putting it together invaluably put me in correspondence with one of the great literary figures of the century, albeit one not always regarded as such. We sold a British edition to Lawrence & Wishart, the Communist Party publishers. They took three hundred initially – a small number but it helped us a lot. They could take that number without having to go to a full board meeting. They sold them all and came back for more, and we ended up printing a paperback edition as well as the initial hardback. We tried to sell an American edition too, and negotiated with the left-wing leaning Humanities Press, but negotiations broke down, ostensibly over a shared imprint.

'How can I put Wild & Woolley on the title page, people would think I'd lost it,' the publisher said.

The success of Jack's book encouraged us to develop further titles in this area. We approached Ric Throssell to assemble a volume of the uncollected essays by his mother, Katharine Susannah Prichard, which appeared in due course as *Straight Left*. I assembled a manuscript of Jack's writings on his father, Norman Lindsay, but this was late in the piece when Wild & Woolley was struggling and in the end we were not able to go ahead with it. Roger Barnes asked to look at the manuscript, and I never saw it again. I also commissioned a collection of the literary essays of John Anderson, the Sydney University philosopher who had been so influential in the mid-century, and whose spirit was still invoked by the Libertarians. By the time it was completed Wild & Woolley had changed its direction and I was no longer involved: the manuscript was directed across to Hale & Iremonger, who in due course published it. The essays turned out to be rather dated and dull, but as Brian Kiernan remarked, at least their collection brought to an end Anderson's much touted reputation as a significant critic of literature.

It was a pity not to have published Jack's essays on Norman Lindsay. Jack was one of the great creative minds of the twentieth century. His output was phenomenal – more than 150 books of poetry, fiction, biography, history and cultural criticism. The son of Norman's first marriage to

Katie Parkinson, he grew up in Brisbane and took a first in classics at the University of Queensland. Studies of classical Greek and Roman culture were to be a substantial part of his literary production. Determined to be a writer, he set off to Sydney in pursuit of his father. His early work was very much part of Norman's Vitalist, Nietzschean project. Jack edited *Vision*, a literary magazine that promulgated Norman's anti-modernism and included Kenneth Slessor and R. D. FitzGerald among its contributors. The bohemian milieu of those early years is lovingly evoked in his autobiography *The Roaring Twenties*, the cafés, parties, romances, betrayals, evictions, midnight flits and eager, earnest discussions of art and society. It was a world haunted by living legends, Brennan like a 'defeated eagle', Lawson with 'yearning melancholy eyes', deaf and inaudible.

In 1926 Jack went to England where he set up Fanfrolico Press, begun with John Kirtley in Sydney and now continued with P. R. Stephensen and Brian Penton. The press specialised in hand-printed, limited editions of titles that would appeal to the curiosa market. Jack translated the *Satyricon*, *The Golden Ass* and the poems of Catullus, and Norman provided illustrations.

In the 1930s he began to write a series of novels on Roman life – *Cressida's First Lover*, *Rome for Sale* and *Last Days with Cleopatra* among them. His deepening understanding of historical and social processes and his perception of the world crisis led to a decisive break with Norman and a disciplined focus for the great release of his creative energies that ensued. His study of John Bunyan in 1937 was a landmark, one of the first sustained Marxist readings in English of a major literary figure, and he followed it with studies of Charles Dickens and George Meredith.

Jack had always seen himself as a poet and his first published volume was poetry, *Fauns and Ladies*. His new sense of participation with the progressive elements of human society led to his innovative and strikingly successful activist public poetry, the mass declarations *Who are the English?* and *On Guard for Spain*. His later elegy 'Last Words with Dylan Thomas' is one of the great elegies of all time. Throughout his life he continued to write poetry, making a point, he told me, of writing a poem to go along with the dedication in each of his books. His novels included a series focused on revolutionary moments in English history, *Sue Verney*, *1649*, *Men of Forty-Eight* and *Fires in Smithfield*. These were followed with a series on contemporary Britain, notably *Betrayed Spring*, *The Rising Tide* and *All on the Never-Never*, which was turned into a movie.

Despite the hostile climate of the Cold War years, two publishers stood by him, he told me. One was Nicholson at the Bodley Head, who published his autobiographical trilogy. I was later to suggest to Brian Johns that it should be reissued, and it duly appeared in one magnificent volume from Penguin Australia. The other was Tony Adams, first at

Frederick Muller and later with his own imprints. Adams encouraged Jack to write the series of biographies of visual artists that, in his sixties, established yet another reputation for him. His study of Turner was critically acclaimed, and he followed it with volumes on Cézanne, Courbet, Hogarth, Gainsborough and two figures whose work, like Lindsay's, cannot be confined to a single area, William Morris and William Blake. He never returned to Australia. He was always too busy fulfilling book contracts, he said, and could not afford to take time off from writing. He lived by his writing, producing this immense scholarly and creative body of work unsupported by salary, grants or research assistants.

I visited him a number of times at Castle Hedingham in Essex. Commentators occasionally remarked on the irony of an unrepentant Marxist living in a castle. But there was no longer a castle in the village. Jack lived in an old farmhouse whose every wall, every nook, every cranny was lined with books. Yet there was nothing oppressive about this sheer volume of volumes. And Jack's conversation was as voluminous and expansive. He would already be talking when he opened the door to me at midday, and he was as fresh and ready for new topics when I finally collapsed into bed at two in the morning. The ancient world, local history, nuclear physics, political hope, memories of contemporaries like Edith Sitwell and Dylan Thomas – he ranged through all these topics. His interest, his knowledge, his energies were huge and expansive.

Always accessible, approachable, he was extraordinarily generous with his time, both in conversation and correspondence. Apart from occasional vilification, the literary establishment in the main ignored him. When I wrote asking if we could publish his Australian essays the letter came, his wife told me, like a bolt from the blue, a new breath of encouragement. He refused to surrender his commitment to cynicism, despair or defeat. He saw clear-sightedly the cultural and social crisis, yet he was always capable even in the darkest times of seeking out and identifying the positive impulses in individual and social life. His life and work were an enduring inspiration.

Another writer I was in contact with at this time was Christina Stead, but my hopes of publishing her came to nothing. Gerry Wilkes had given me the reissues of Christina's *Seven Poor Men Of Sydney* and *For Love Alone* to review for *Southerly* a decade earlier. That was my first encounter with her. I wrote a long review which was published as an article. Then, in England, 1967–68, *London Magazine* gave me *The Puzzleheaded Girl* and *Cotters' England* to review as they came out. Around that time, Jonah Raskin got in touch with me about a piece I wrote on *Nostromo* for *Essays in Criticism*, and came to stay with me in Woodstock (Oxfordshire, not USA). The visit was cut short when radio news of the disrupted 1968 Democratic convention came through and his wife flew back to demonstrate. Later, she went underground with the Weathermen, and after losing his job at Stony Brook, Jonah became Minister for Information for the Yippies in Algeria, and wrote asking me to join them and Malcolm X whom they had sprung from gaol. I didn't. Anyway, Jonah had interviewed Christina in New York, but whatever US magazine he had sent the interview to had rejected it, so I said, send it to *London Magazine* with which I had a good relationship at the time, and he did, and Alan Ross published it.

I didn't contact Christina Stead myself till I was co-editing an anthology opposing Australian and American involvement in the war in Vietnam, which finally appeared as *We Took Their Orders and Are Dead* (Ure Smith, 1971). She responded to the request to contribute enthusiastically, as had Jack Lindsay, Patrick White and many others, and sent in a piece about her friend Dr Phillip Harvey's Aid to North Viet Nam program. Shortly after she wrote apologising for the bad typing but explained she'd not felt well, and had, it turned out, had a heart attack that day. The man who killed Christina Stead, I reflected with dismay.

Back in England in 1972, I wrote to her again and met her in London and we had lunch with an old friend of hers, Paul Koston, a book distributor. They got into an argument, I forget what about, but he accused her of being a Stalinist and she accused him of being a typical Trotskyite become small businessman. It was a friendly and I think familiar argument. And either that or another time I met Dr Harvey.

For all my anti-war efforts, my interests were primarily literary. I wanted to meet writers and swim in the literary stream so perhaps I was a shade disappointed that Christina seemed to have nothing to do with any literary world.

We kept in touch and after I'd set up Wild & Woolley I sent her copies of books we'd published. She was always interested. Always candid. Hazel Rowley's biography says that Christina's last years were barren and empty and cut off: but that was not true. She engaged with the books I sent her, writing detailed and sometimes lengthy reactions to them. She wrote that she enjoyed *The Short Story Embassy* and read it three times; *Zimmer's Essay*, she wrote, was 'a book that lives in the mind and heart'. She was very responsive to Vicki Viidikas's work. 'As for V. V.,' she wrote to me, 'her portraits of men instant and sharp, could only have been done by a girl who took those chances (and had talent). She has tremendous talent.' In other letters, not in Ron Geering's two-volume selection but now in the National Library of Australia, she responded to *Tabloid Story* and stories in it by Dal Stivens, Peter Carey and myself, to Antigone Kefala, Rudi Krausmann, Jack Lindsay, *Abortion: The Bobigny Affair*, *The Radical Reader*, and to various books of mine I sent her. She asked me to send a set of Wild & Woolley titles in print to the Hawks Nest public library for the memorial shelves to John Dillaway, with whom she had corresponded.

I regretted not having seen more of her when she came back to

Australia in 1974. I visited her a couple of times – I wish now it had been more, but my life was a hectic, overcrowded whirl of publishing, affairs, fiction, editing, teaching, raging on. What I thought of as the literary life. One time we met in a pizzeria and she talked about Spain, USA, etc. But the traffic was loud and she had a low voice so I couldn't hear most of what she said. I remember asking her if she and Bill Blake, her husband, had gone to Spain to support the Republicans in the civil war.

'No, no,' she said, 'it was before the war.'

Bill's banking employer Alf Hurst had got the idea that with the Republic there would be a lot of land going cheaply, all the aristocratic big landowners fleeing and selling out.

'It was one of his money-making schemes,' she said.

'Did it work?' I asked.

'No, no,' she said.

She told me her American publisher visited them in Spain and read *House Of All Nations* and requested a rewrite but she couldn't face it and refused to revise; he published it anyway. It is one of the great exposés of banking and finance capitalism, based on Bill Blake's experiences working with Alf Hurst and others, an always pertinent account of the causes behind the system's recurrent economic crises. She told me to read Ralph Fox, her good friend who was killed in the Spanish Civil War, said what a horrible person Koestler was, and in response to my questions, denied that she and Bill had left the USA because of McCarthyite persecution in the 1950s.

Another time I visited her in the shed-like building at her brother's house that she lived in. We were supposed to go for lunch at a fish restaurant near Tom Ugly's Bridge but she felt unwell, angina, couldn't manage it, insisted my girlfriend and I went anyway, insisted on paying I think, gave my girlfriend a cookbook she no longer had any use for ('everything I like is bad for me'), gave me one of Bill Blake's novels if I promised to read it.

Then on a visit to New York she had a heart attack, and rumour was that it was an expensive hospitalisation, aren't they all in America? When she returned I suggested that she apply for a Literature Board Fellowship, to assemble, say, a collection of interviews she had given, which we would publish with Wild & Woolley. The fellowship would raise some money, even if the book sales didn't. I'd spoken to someone at the Literature Board and discussed this with them, as a way of helping Christina to pay for the US hospital bills. It seemed a simple notional project that wouldn't involve her in much work. Indeed I could have collated the interviews, articles and scattered reviews. But she was resolutely against it. I thought she was being excessively punctilious, but she no doubt had her reasons.

'No, no,' she said.

There were a number of interviews that I knew of. There was Jonah's interview from *London Magazine*. And she had done a radio interview for the ABC with Anne Whitehead and Anne included it as an appendix to her MA thesis which I examined, and I persuaded Laurie Hergenhan to publish it in *Australian Literary Studies*. And there were others. But she was adamant.

'I regret them all.'

I suggested she applied for a fellowship to collect her book reviews and travel articles.

'No, no,' she said, 'you apply, you get it.'

I didn't want it. She didn't want it. So it didn't happen.

I lost touch for a while after this, change and disruption in my own life. I was a bit miffed she wouldn't accept my charitable offer of taxpayers' money, I think.

There was another occasion we met, I remember now. She asked me would I drive her and Elizabeth Harrower up to Palm Beach where Bryan Westwood was painting her portrait – lots of tiny sea creatures round the edge and Christina amidst them. She felt she needed moral support while she sat for it. Westwood had recently painted the infamous Sir John Kerr, who'd posed without his judicial wig, technically not yet inaugurated as a judge or something but, Westwood said, he suspected it was because he was vain about his mane of silver hair. So we spent the day at Palm Beach.

Then Lorna Tracy and Jon Silkin planned a Stead issue for *Stand*.

They asked would I interview her. Again I was swamped with work, didn't think I could manage the technology of recording, or get anyone to transcribe an interview, didn't think interviewing was part of the writer's self-image I was assembling. I asked a university colleague, Giulia Giuffré, if she would do it. She'd recently interviewed another venerable Australian woman writer.

'You could do a series,' I said, 'maybe a book, interview them while they're still alive.'

She did – interview Christina, and other women writers, and in due course produced a valuable book.

I phoned Christina to arrange the interview and we talked a while.

'I'd like to see you,' she said.

But when I phoned to arrange to visit, the family said it wasn't possible. I didn't know why. I never did see her again. I regret that. Not seeing more of her. Not that it really matters. Writers write. You meet them in their books. Any time you want to.

The *Australian Book Review* asked me to review Hazel Rowley's biography, and I happily agreed to. I'd talked to her when she was writing it, guardedly, as I had talked to Christina's earlier biographer Chris Williams. Rowley's book appalled me with its portrayal of Christina as a 'monster' which she certainly wasn't. I sent in my review and *ABR* published it. They added a favourable review to balance it in the same issue. Some time later Debra Adelaide attacked me in the

Australian Author alleging I'd asked to review the book (I hadn't) and that I was hostile to the biography because I felt I owned Stead.

No more than Christina was I into 'owning' things. I was not a defender of private property, ownership. I'd written one article and a handful of reviews of her work, that was all. If anything my feelings were delight that anyone should write about her work, and guilt that I hadn't written more about her. When Geoffrey Dutton had asked me to write on her for the revised *Pelican History Of Australian Literature* I regretfully, and guiltily, declined: I was overburdened with work – teaching, writing, publishing, committed to a couple of unfulfilled contracts on Marcus Clarke. I couldn't see how I'd ever find time to read and digest and write intelligently on all those substantial novels of hers. Her novels were not on any university course at that time – so no way could I duplicate anything I wrote for lectures or seminars.

Later, I tried to assuage that guilt by writing an article on her novellas for a festschrift for Leslie Rogers – the thing about festschrifts is that you have a better chance of publishing something in them than getting an article that you have sent unsolicited to a journal accepted. Then I lectured on her when her work finally appeared on the Australian Literature course at Sydney, and drew on the lecture for one of the Colin Roderick lectures I was asked to give in 1992. I still feel I should have written more. Maybe I still can. Though I find it harder and harder to write literary criticism. But one good thing did come out of the Hazel

Rowley book. She attacked Christina for her wickedness in taking letters written to her by her father, and incorporating them unchanged into *The Man Who Loved Children*. That's an interesting idea, I thought. So I dug out letters Christina had sent me and used them as a basis for a story, 'I Like Him To Write', in which I tried to capture something of my memories of her. Jenny Lee published it in *Meanjin* and I collected it in *This is For You.*

The Wild & Woolley non-fiction list made sense in the context of the culture of the times. English Literature was the dominant subject in the humanities, and it was under challenge. Its narrow boundaries were being opened up to move beyond those so-called 'purely literary values', whatever they were, that the academy espoused, and to include a more politically aware criticism – like Jack Lindsay's essays – and a consideration of popular culture and mass media. The intellectual ferment generated by the anti-Vietnam war movement had encouraged us to look at the nature of the discipline as it was taught, to ask why it was so resistant to expanding its horizons and so committed to refusing the political. Together with a colleague in the English Department, Stephen Knight, I was caught up in this radicalising movement at the university, indeed we positioned ourselves in the vanguard of it.

I was talking about Stephen only the other day to Pat Woolley.

She was very impressed with Stephen's television manner in a documentary he made on Shakespeare.

'Shakespeare?' I asked, not recalling Stephen active in Shakespeare studies, wide ranging and all as he is.

'Yeah, *Hamlet* or something,' she said.

'Robin Hood?' I suggested tentatively.

'Yeah. Robin Hood,' she agreed. One of those *Classics Illustrated*.

Stephen as television presenter was a far cry from the young man I knew in the 1970s, the lapels of his leather jacket glued down with Araldite to keep them in place. Or the even younger man Lee Cataldi, Alison Cunningham and I drove up to Cairns in a VW with in 1963, a five-day trip each way. Each night he lay in his sleeping bag reading the Bible. I found it disturbing. Was he secretly a Christian? Was it really background for his doctorate on *Piers Plowman*, as he claimed? Why wasn't he relaxing with crime fiction?

By the time he moved to reading, and writing about, crime fiction, in which he became something of a critical authority, I found that disturbing too. Why wasn't he reading literary fiction, the sort we were publishing with Wild & Woolley?

Probably on principle. These were the years in which Stephen proposed the idea of a trade union for fictional characters, or, rather, for their originals, with threats of strike action if proper working conditions, financial rewards and pension plans were not instituted.

He felt the writers down at the pub were getting characters too cheaply.

I remember when a photographer, Richard Harris, came to the pub, the Newcastle, to take cover shots for my first book. Stephen warned me there was an ASIO or special branch agent photographing people at the bar. He refused to believe my explanation. He ensured he kept out of shot. He was not the only one. No one I knew appeared on the cover, they were all hiding.

These were the years of the anti-Vietnam war movement. We were both in the front line of one rally, the provocateurs behind trying to get us to break down the doors of some university building. Do I recall Stephen using his rugby playing skills and flying at the door with his shoulder? Or letting down the tyres of the police car nearby? I can't remember. Those were the 1960s and, as they always say, anyone who remembers the 60s wasn't there.

Stephen instituted a series of seminars, extra-curricular, that looked at some of the more politicised literary-critical issues of the times. It was not restricted to English students, not restricted to students. Carl Harrison-Ford, disenrolled from his doctoral studies, and his partner Cassandra Pybus, then a History graduate student, used to come along regularly. So did Lee Cataldi, teaching at Tempe High at this time. I dutifully attended for the semester or so that the seminars ran.

From this we moved on to the idea of a collection of oppositional critical essays, which emerged as *The Radical Reader* in 1977. It was a separate impulse from Wild & Woolley. Wild & Woolley I still thought of primarily as a publisher of new fiction, despite the poets. *The Radical Reader* was a continuation of that movement begun with opposition to the Vietnam war, and part of my engagement with my day job. But since Wild & Woolley existed, it seemed sensible to publish the collection through Wild & Woolley, rather than independently; and no other publisher seemed likely to want to risk it.

According to Carl Harrison-Ford, who was packing orders at this time, he went into the warehouse early one morning, or was it late one night, to find a box of *Radical Readers* on fire. No great damage was done, and perhaps because of that, I could never get my mind around the issue. Hot books, but hardly that inflammatory. Local kids breaking in, perhaps, but why select that title? It made no sense and I forgot about it.

'I hope there are more *Radical Readers*!' Christina Stead wrote to me. The first one did well and we planned a second volume. For some reason – cost, maybe – it was being typeset in Indonesia where someone either Stephen or Pat knew was running a development program and had begun a typesetting operation. But either a fire or a flood or a riot destroyed the typeset copy. We tried again, but the second attempt was lost in the fire that engulfed the new warehouse that Pat had leased in downtown Sydney.

In the end Stephen recycled the materials as a basis for *Words and*

Worlds which he co-edited with Soumyen Mukherjee in 1983. By the time the volume appeared, some of the original contributions had been withdrawn and published elsewhere, and of those contributors who remained, some substituted different essays.

But it marked the beginning of another radical initiative on campus, the publishing project *Sydney Studies in Society and Culture*, with which I was associated and through which we in due course published over twenty volumes.

The University of Sydney historian Soumyen Mukherjee had been instrumental in setting up the Sydney Association for Studies in Society and Culture. The aim had been to provide a cross-disciplinary forum so that literary critics, historians, anthropologists and social scientists could meet and discuss issues that extended beyond the narrow boundaries of their departments. Departmental boundaries were as closely guarded in those days as any contemporary border security operation. It wouldn't do to have political scientists talking to literary types, historians getting together with political scientists. The association confronted these taboos and arranged talks, seminars and conferences. The proceedings of the conferences were to be published. Hence the publishing project, Sydney Studies.

Wild & Woolley had shown how it was possible to set up a small press and do some significant and successful publishing. There had always been something of a tradition of scholarly specialist presses. A number of academic series now sprang up. Wild & Woolley distributed David Myers' study of Patrick White's short stories, *The Peacocks and the Bourgeoisie*, published by the Adelaide University Union Press. Small press series on Australian literature were established by committed, enthusiastic and entrepreneurial academics in the University of Western Australia, Monash University, James Cook University, the University of New England and elsewhere.

I was a member of the Sydney Association and helped with the first volume. After that the conferences got going and five volumes of proceedings were published. By this time Sydney University Press had been closed down, along with many other Australian university presses. Governmental policy had led to the running down of the humanities, staff numbers were dramatically dropping, student enrolments were drastically reduced, as the new world order directed the young into economics, law, business studies and computer science. Not only were the university presses closed down: traditional commercial scholarly publishers began to shy away from the humanities because the market had become so small.

Around 1990 I became chair of the Association and we began publishing original books alongside conference proceedings. Monographs they were called in those days. I remember the arts editor of Cambridge University Press expressing surprise and admiration, the former especially, for what we were doing. Four hundred copies was now the expected sale of a work of literary criticism, he told me. Internationally. Not long afterwards Craig Munro of University of Queensland Press told me two hundred copies were as many as you might expect to sell of a book on Australian literature.

We used to print a thousand copies and sold most of them. The money received from conference enrolments and the association's membership was used to fund the books. When conferences became fewer and we published more original monographs, we sought subsidies from the university, the Australian Academy of the Humanities and such like sources. Any profits made on individual books went back into the bank account to fund the next titles. No one got paid. The authors received no royalties, though they were given lots of free copies to send to colleagues in their fields, spread the word, get reviews, hand out as Christmas presents. None of us took any money for the time spent on the myriad tasks of commissioning and writing readers' reports, editing, proof-reading and publishing. It was all very hand to mouth. I would meet Ed Lidums, the printer, in the university staff club and hand over camera-ready copy. I would deliver the books to our distributor in Leichhardt, Paul Brennan's Primavera Press, in the boot of my car.

Over twenty-two years we published twenty-two titles. We received excellent reviews, in scholarly journals, the *Times Literary Supplement*, the *Australian* and *Australian Book Review.* We arranged co-publishing in the United Kingdom and India. And then it all came to an end. The reforms in tax law, the introduction of the GST, and the ABN, made it all unfeasible. None of us had the time, energy or expertise to comply with the requirements of quarterly reporting, of audited accounts. Nor could we afford to pay to have these tasks done. The whole operation was run on a shoestring.

And so, regretfully, we decided to call it a day, pack it in, close down the Association, take early retirement. The university staff club where we met the printer had already been closed down. Sydney Studies in Society and Culture came to an end.

In large part this was a consequence of new governmental legislation. Much has been said about the law of unintended consequences. A political action in one area produces unfortunate consequences in another. Governmental requirements had made a centuries-old tradition of voluntary activity impossible to sustain. Voluntarism was now to be replaced by professionalism: except that in many cases it was not replaced, it simply ceased to exist.

I remembered a report from England. The drum and pipe band that had performed at a village Remembrance Day ceremony for nearly forty years had been closed down. Health and Safety regulations insisted on a higher proportion of adults to children than the band could guarantee. Charles Moore remarked in the *Spectator* (27 October 2007) on 'how painful regulation is for any organisation which exists on a thin margin.

It is the natural condition of most small local societies to lack money, legal expertise, clerical time and spare bodies.'

Are these unintended consequences? Or is it all part of the remorseless imposition of control and monopolisation on every aspect of individual life? Large organisations, major commercial enterprises, can absorb the cost of quarterly reporting, auditing, health and safety, environmental and other government requirements. But voluntary organisations, small presses, little magazines, and learned societies are gradually being squeezed out of existence. The amateur and the voluntary are being replaced by the professional, the global, the corporate.

This is especially the case in scholarly publishing, which insofar as it survives is being increasingly driven into the control of global monopolies. As Colin Steele wrote in the *Australian* (Higher Education, 31 October 2007), 'In 2006, 20 publishers accounted for 84 per cent of revenues of the $US11 billion publishing market in science, technology and medicine. The top five STM publishers account for 50 per cent of the market. Who loses? Smaller publishers, academic societies and academic monograph publishing.'

Sydney Studies was one of the publishing projects that lost. Its demise was symptomatic of the way the variety of our cultural and political expression is being reduced. Sometimes you have to wonder whether this is not an unintended consequence at all, but part of an overriding plan.

Among various previous activities, Pat Woolley included dress-designing. Involvement in a range of magazines, from that first, duplicated, unofficial magazine at school, to the more recent and still going, *Tabloid Story*, ensured that I had my own experience in design, too.

The body of the text Pat set on the IBM composer. After the first two volumes, we decided against justifying the right-hand margins. Justifying involved a further manual process, took more time; but apart from that the spacing always had a tendency to look a bit windy, rivers of white space snaking down the page, the gaps between words erratic and sometimes excessive. It looked better when the copy was set ragged-right and consistently letter-spaced, so that was what we did after the first two titles. I don't recall anyone ever remarking on it. But for those who did notice, it gave a sense of the new, a new style for a new technology, that went along with publishing directly into paperback.

I had my own design preferences. Economy to begin with. Why not, I speculated, save the cost of four-colour printing by doing black and white colours? The two American small presses whose work we represented and who were in the forefront of *avant-garde* literary publishing, City Lights and New Directions, had successfully followed this policy for two decades or more. Amidst all the garish, four-colour, over-designed book jackets screaming out 'Buy me, buy me' in the shops, black and white covers were strikingly distinctive.

Our first Wild & Woolley covers were black-and-white. (Except for Silkin's poems which were black and blue). Later I was persuaded it was not much more expensive to run a second colour, so there we went. And eventually it was four colours and in the end Pat and I spent hours huffing and puffing at each other about cover art, and paying artists. A dozen years later, when Bob Adamson and Minas Poulos and I established Paper Bark Press, I got my way with black-and-white covers; but this was largely because Bob's partner was a photographer, Judo Gemes. She had exhibited with Yoko Ono and came out of that art tradition that was committed to black-and-white, rejecting colour photography as somehow unartistic, commercial or something. So Paper Bark ran with black and white photographic covers for years. And looked good.

Pat and I had our strong opinions about design, and we knew a few artists and photographers. Over time we had cover art and photography by David Aspden, David Bromley, Ron Cobb, Aleks Danko, William Fish, Richard Harris, Bruce Petty, Martin Sharp, Wes Stacey, Brett Whiteley and more.

Rudi Krausmann had the idea of interspersing the pieces of his collection with pen and ink drawings by Brett Whiteley. Whiteley was supposed to be a selling point. The drawings had been done separately and seemed to have no necessary connection with the writings. But Rudi and Brett seemed happy with that. Pat and I made some sort of selection. We had to go along to a gallery and have an audience with the artist. He handed over a box of photographic reproductions. He insisted the cover should have some colour, just one spot of colour, he stressed, any colour, anywhere. We disregarded him. We were still committed to black-and-white covers at this stage. As soon as the book was printed, Rudi insisted that we should go round to visit Brett and show it to him. The books were still hot from the press, pretty well literally, and the glue of the so-called perfect binding had not yet set. Roger Barnes the printer was reluctant for us to take copies away, the glue needed to set for twenty-four hours. But Rudi was adamant. Unlike the glue. Brett set about gracing them with his signature. He bent a copy back firmly, in that philistine way that people do who either have no feeling for books, or outright hostility to them, the binding snapped, and the pages fell loose. He was most put out.

I have never been quite sure about design. The very name carries the implication of manipulation, of someone having designs on you. Between writers and editors on the one hand, and designers on the other, there is likely to be a constant battle. Designers like layout, pictures, white space. Writers, and most editors, like words. Writers like to get a lot of words onto the page. Designers like a lot of white space or display typography or illustrations, and often all three.

'A picture's worth a thousand words,' the cartoonist Bruce Petty used to say to me cheerfully. I was not amused.

My first experience of designers was in editing *Isis*, the weekly student magazine at Oxford, back in 1962. I was from the beginning lobbied by a couple of designers. No one lobbied me more insistently, unless it was the political activists of CND, the Committee for Nuclear Disarmament, who managed to slip an article or news item on nuclear disarmament into every issue. The two designers were by contrast apparently unpolitical. One, Jonathan Green-Armytage, later became a designer on that elegant magazine *Queen*. He was a charming, languid man, who once asked his tutor if it was all right for him to go to Bath. The tutor assumed it was an issue of personal hygiene and happily said yes, when in fact it was a matter of spending a weekend away from university. The other was Laurence Reed, of the Austin Reed tailoring family, who had served in the navy in the Pacific and gave me photographs he had taken of atomic bomb explosions, thereby no doubt putting me in breach of the Official Secrets Act and supplementing the campaign plans of CND when we published them. These two designers pressured me endlessly for more white space, more photographs, more display, while I resisted cutting an article just to accommodate the look of things. It was all an educative experience.

The problem with design is that it comes at a cost. In *Editor*, his account of editing the English *Daily Telegraph*, Max Hastings indicated his own uneasiness about the way contemporary design reduced the number of stories the paper could fit in. He compared a random day in 1987 with one in 2001. 'The front page carried eight stories in 2001 against seventeen in 1987; page 2 had five against sixteen; page three ran three stories against ten in 1987; page 4, five stories against sixteen ...The triumph of the packagers, the design kings, has imposed a cost, especially on the margins of foreign coverage.'

The other cost is the cost in dollars and cents. The editor of a recent collection of short stories told me that permission for the cover art for the volume was initially billed at $1000. In comparison most contributors were receiving $200–$300. On top of the permission for the art, is the payment for the designer to incorporate it into a design – another $500–$1000. Time and again it seems to the writer, especially to the not especially commercial novelist or poet, that the designer is being paid more than the author.

It was not always like this. I can remember when the front page of *The Times* consisted entirely of classified advertisements. Even then, that seemed somewhat extreme and archaic. But the early Penguin books were a masterpiece of standardised design. Penguin have now reissued some titles in that format. A block of colour, just one colour, top and bottom, and the title and author's name in straightforward typography. It meant that these pioneering paperbacks could be produced cheaply. There was no need to pay an artist and a designer for each title. There was no need to spend time or money thinking about design, once the template was established. The hardback publishers of those years were often similarly economical. Victor Gollancz's books were always in the same matt yellow jacket, with a distinctive typeface announcing the title and author, and no illustration. Faber and Faber had a modernist, sans serif typeface, maybe a couple of colours, but again a standard design. Oxford University Press books had pale blue matt paper wrappers, and standard black lettering.

With Wild & Woolley, some of the fiercest arguments Pat and I had were about cover designs. We would sweat and fume and rant and rage for hours on end. And then it struck me that we were wasting days in futile worrying about a small press poetry title that would probably be lucky to sell 200 copies. The cover design was not going to make much difference. Maybe it would make a difference if we could get the book into a bookshop chain, but increasingly that was becoming a problem for an independent small press. Design, I decided, was something of a fetish.

They still produce those simple covers in France and other parts of Europe. Plain matte paper covers, a red border, and simply clean typography in black, or black and red, for the title and the author's name. I followed that style later for the Sydney Studies series. In Australia, like the rest of the English-speaking world, things have generally changed. Yet I still wonder whether cover design makes much difference to the sales of a book. Most books in bookshops are displayed spine outwards. Only a small number get to be laid out flat on a display table. Of course, some designers have begun to put illustrations on the spine, when the book is fat enough. This is presumably another reason why popular fiction is getting longer and bulkier.

But sometimes I wonder if design is not just the equivalent of another stealth tax, an added layer of cost to things, like bridge tolls and motorway tolls and parking meters and airport departure taxes and GST and land tax and bank charges, that make the contemporary world such an expensive place to live in.

By the mid-1970s, most of the independent book distributors had been absorbed by the larger publishers. And distributors, those that survived, took another 22 per cent of the retail cost of a book, on top of the 40 per cent the bookshops took. It didn't leave a lot, after you had paid a 10 per cent author's royalty. That was why we had to do our own distributing.

Early on Pat acquired a tiny little two-stroke Honda van from the car dealership in Bega her mother and stepfather ran, a trade-in painted with the name of a NSW south coast laundry and the slogan 'Let our phone line be your clothes line'. We left it overnight in the university grounds and the campus police impounded it, thinking it was stolen. There were not many vehicles like it around and it attracted notice. When it died, we acquired another one like it, this one unpainted. So Pat got the artist Aleks Danko to re-paint it. He was

a very contemporary painter, and he painted the sides so they looked like graffiti.

Wild & Woolley, it announced in bright red. Urgent Book Delivery.

Like those medical couriers blazoned with Urgent Blood Delivery signs.

In explanation we added, 'A good book is the precious lifeblood of a master spirit', Milton's definition from *Areopagitica*. It got us into Column Eight of the *Sydney Morning Herald* and maybe that even sold some books.

Publishing until the development of the e-book depended pretty much on bookshops. A huge percentage of published books rarely appeared in bookshops, of course; they were sold directly to libraries, or had their own specialist niche markets. But for a general publishing list such as we had with Wild & Woolley, the bookshops were essential. I had always loved bookshops, and Sydney has always had some delightful ones.

A decade earlier when I first arrived in Sydney and after Germaine had organised my life and got her boyfriend, the harpsichordist and philosopher Paul Thom, to drive us round while she found me a kettle and a teapot and a flat in the Cross, one of the first things I did was go out and discover a bookshop. When I say discover, that is not to imply the shop was ever lost. Back then it was certainly known to those in the know. But it was a discovery for me. Years later people would tell me in reverential tones that Patrick White shopped there. Those were the years when people still spoke of authors, or at least of Patrick White, in reverential tones. I am not sure they even used the word shopped. This was a shrine to literature, an amazing treasure house of quality and exotica, not a trading post, and for years I used to pore over its delights.

The proprietor was dignified and ladylike, a figure from a past era vanishing even then amidst the strip clubs and developing sleaze of the Cross. It was known as Clay's bookshop and I vaguely thought of her as Miss Clay, while knowing that wasn't her name and wondering if it was called that because it was situated in Macleay Street. It wasn't named after Patrick White's story 'Clay,' surely? For years she presided there, Norma Chapman, one of the great characters of the Sydney booksellers' world. She was one of the booksellers who stocked our books.

Bookshops in Sydney sometimes performed more diverse roles than simply selling books. Among the many memorable characters of the Sydney booksellers' world we dealt with was Alec Sheppard, or Colonel Sheppard as he was generally known. Minas Poulos, indeed, referred to him simply as The Colonel, *tout court*. He had been an officer in military intelligence in Greece in World War II, and could sometimes appear to be the archetypal caricature of the moustached colonel. But he was far from that. I had got to know him in the mid-1960s in the early years of the Vietnam war, and the protests that it generated, when I had obtained the English pamphlet, *Vietnam Briefing*, outlining objections to the American involvement in the war in Vietnam, and was looking for ways to publish it in Australia now that Australia had joined in the war. Details about what was really going on, what the war was really all about, were hard to find. I talked to Hugh Price, then the manager of Sydney University Press, and he put me in touch with the Colonel, and with remarkably little fuss the Colonel published the pamphlet under the imprint of Morgan's, his bookshop in Bathurst Street. That was the sort of Quixotic thing booksellers used to do, support causes, publish controversial pamphlets that the established publishers avoided. Later he was deeply involved in the court action to make D. H. Lawrence's *Lady*

Chatterley's Lover available after years of being banned. It was a crucial event in bringing Australia into the modern age after the repressions of the 1950s. It was one of the factors that enabled Wild & Woolley to publish and import the sorts of books that we dealt with, something that would have been impossible a decade earlier.

The opening of Abbey's bookshop in the Queen Victoria Building had been in its own way the opening of an era. 1968. I had returned to Australia to find that Abbey's was the place that all the writers were talking about. Amidst the inadequate sameness of the old colonial bookstores, Abbey's was a site of excitement and discovery. Suddenly there it was with a range of hitherto inaccessible literary treasures. Piles of recent American *avant-garde* remainders, direct imports from the United Kingdom of the rarer literary titles, small-press treasures, the exotic and esoteric. It attracted the poets like wasps to a sugar press, not something Ron or Eve Abbey always appreciated. One time Ron rang up the books editor of the *Sydney Morning Herald,* to complain that one of their reviewers had been stealing books and had run out of the shop when they tried to apprehend him. That was Martin Johnston, in dispute with his publisher, stealing copies of his own book of poems to present to friends, or maybe to supply to reviewers. Martin, of course, was a literary treasure in himself, the son of the writers George Johnston and Charmian Clift, and a character in an Elizabeth Jane Howard novel set on Hydra.

Abbey's not only had splendid literary stock and splendid literary customers, but also employed some splendid literary figures. One of them was Vicki Viidikas, who could be fearsome. Once some wretched academic approached her and asked did they give a discount on purchases to university teachers.

She fixed him with a contemptuous eye and a scathing tongue. 'I think lecturers get away with enough already without giving them discounts as well,' she snarled.

Jim Thorburn's Pocket Bookshop was another treasure site; those were the days of the sudden expansion of quality paperback publishing, and Jim stocked an enticing range of literature and politics and psychology. He seemed a classic dour Glaswegian, but could open up into enthusiastic debate and discussion. It was in 1972 in his basement shop in King Street that my first book of stories had been launched, the first title in Frank Thompson's pioneering fiction list for University of Queensland Press. UQP, with a $750 grant from the Literature Board, hired Pat to launch and promote their next three titles in Jim's new Clarence Street shop – my *Living Together*, Peter Carey's *The Fat Man in History* and Geoff Wyatt's *The Tidal Forest*. Bookshop launches were not an everyday event at that time: it was all new and exciting. Later launches got more out of control. Peter Carey and I signed copies of each other's books at a launch at William de Winton's New Edition shop in Paddington, I remember, along with increasingly ribald personalised inscriptions. I still remember the look of terror on some innocent shopper's face as she came in unawares to buy a book, and the assembled literati tried to cajole her into having a drink and who knows what else. I remember Pat becoming increasingly incensed when she suspected Bob Debus of going round this or some other launch poaching our authors for Angus & Robertson or UQP, whoever he was working for at the time. Would a future state and federal minister – Prisons, Police, Home Affairs – really do such a thing? What on earth could he have been poaching, anyway?

By Carey's next launch things had changed, and not for the better. I can't remember now whether the event was at the University Co-op bookshop in Bay Street, Broadway, or at Gleebooks in Glebe Point Road. But wherever it was, formal entertainment was provided in the shape of Max Gillies reading a play script by Barry Oakley. We were all expected to listen. I withdrew to the kitchen for a quiet smoke and a talk together with the University of Queensland Press rep, but even that was deemed unacceptable and Barry ordered us to keep quiet and pay attention. He seemed very stern and schoolmasterly; but it was in advertising that he and Peter had worked together, as an engaging memoir of them in their early years by Morris Lurie makes clear. Perhaps they were concerned to insert the values of that business into the world of books. Many would say they succeeded. It certainly looked like the beginning of the end of book launches for fun and their transformation into commercial productions

with speeches, dramatisations and the extraordinary requirement that you pay for the book. No longer freebies, but niche marketing.

As for Gleebooks, there was that unfortunate episode where my wife-to-be asked, 'Do you have any of Michael Wilding's books?'

'Yes, unfortunately,' said the assistant.

At which, she said, she picked up some convenient instrument, maybe a *New York Review of Books,* rolled it into a cylinder, and loyally delivered a blow to the top of his head. At least I hope it was the somewhat limp *New York Review* and not a sturdy volume of the *Shorter Oxford Dictionary on Historical Principles.* It was quite a while before I felt game to enter Gleebooks again. But I forgave them. I only hope they reciprocated.

New shops continued to appear and it was all a ferment of excitement: Philip Bray in Darling Street, Balmain, who despite Nigel Roberts' repeated and public cajoling seemed reluctant to stock the works of the local Balmain writers; Susumu Hirayanagi and Nicholas Pounder at Exiles in Taylor Square, who stocked most of our list and imports: Lesley McKay's at Double Bay. And of course all the Melbourne and Canberra and Newcastle bookshops. These were the rounds Pat and I made for Wild & Woolley, those were the shops.

In those days it was still possible to start a small press and go round the bookshops and appeal to the booksellers' decency, love of literature, altruism and anything else that came to mind until, often perhaps in desperation to get you to leave, they agreed to order copies. It was not a task I enjoyed, painful, gruelling, potentially humiliating. Pat did most of it. In the end we realised it was something at which we were not especially good. Haranguing booksellers on their wickedness in not stocking your titles was not the way to go, though Pat was developing quite a powerful tirade. I am sure that the booksellers were vastly relieved when we got ourselves our rep, Minas Poulos. He took our books around in a cool, relaxed sort of way.

'Think of them as furnishings,' he told the booksellers. 'See them as providing a literary décor,' he said of our new Australian writing and imported American *avant-garde* lists, 'it gives a touch of quality.'

And once the books got into the shops and displayed, then people did indeed buy them. We were very grateful to those bookshops that bought our furnishings. The Bridge, the Opera House, the harbour, the beaches, these are the things you always think of when you think about Sydney. But never forget the bookshops, and what a crucial part of Sydney they have been. Especially if you are a writer or a publisher.

It was not just a matter of publishing books, it was also a way of life, a scene as we called it. Activities were not simply commercial activities. They were also a focus for meeting, socialising, raging on. We made the most of the events, book launches, readings, interstate and overseas visitors, as a way of attracting media attention, and having a party.

Bob Adamson was a great activist and enthusiast for poetry, something other poets readily recognised. At the Adelaide Festival one year he had talked to Allen Ginsberg, and Ginsberg had said to him, 'The poet you ought to be in touch with is Robert Duncan'. Bob found Duncan's works, absorbed them, entered into correspondence with him, and in due course Bob and Cheryl brought Duncan out to Australia. Various readings were organised, I arranged for him to give a couple of talks at the university, and in the course of these activities

Nigel Roberts obtained a 'prepuce' from Duncan for his *In Casablanca For the Waters.* While I was a member of the Literature Board at this time the New Zealand Arts Council wrote that they were funding a visit by Robert Creeley. It seemed sensible to bring him to Australia, too, he was another influential proponent of contemporary American poetry. Neither Duncan nor Creeley were published by presses we represented, but their presence was all part of that American *avant-garde* that was so influential on the younger Australian writers at that time. It all contributed to the excitement, the scene. Anyway, many of Creeley's works were available from the remainder trays at Abbeys and Gould's Third World Bookshop. I remember Carl Harrison-Ford brought a swag of them into my room at university and got Creeley to autograph them for his collection. It was quite a considerable swag. 'You checking my signature?' said Creeley suspiciously. He would only sign so many at a time. Maybe he would have been more enthusiastic had Carl removed the bargain price stickers from them. It was the American Bicentennial year, 1976, and Tom Shapcott had edited an anthology of Australian and American Poetry. It was launched at the Seymour Centre and Creeley turned up. Shapcott asked him would he launch it, or say a few words. Creeley looked through the book, found his work was not represented, and declined. We met him again in Bolinas on one of our American visits and at a party late one night he proposed hiring a car and heading across America. 'Drive,' he might have said. But we didn't.

We aimed at getting known, getting press attention, spreading the word. And it worked. We got excellent press coverage. And we got coverage in the literary journals too. Jon Silkin returned to England happy with his visit, despite that near-death experience in Pittwater. We came up with the idea of a special issue of *Stand* devoted to the new Australian writing, and it duly appeared. *Stand* was a significant international journal, and this issue was an important part of our global campaign. And then one evening Laurie Hergenhan was visiting from Queensland. Laurie, as well as editing *Australian Literary Studies*, enjoyed the ambience of literary life: he appreciated not just the past achievements of Australian writing, but also the contemporary ferment, happily observing us in our bohemian disarray, whose continuity he could trace back through the roaring twenties, the Lindsays, the *Bulletin*, Lawson and the nineties, to Marcus Clarke, Adam Lindsay Gordon and Henry Kendall in Melbourne's Yorick Club of the 1860s. 'What you should do,' we told him, the success of *Stand*'s special issue fresh in our minds, 'is a special issue of *Australian Literary Studies*.' And he did. It was a brave, indeed an historic, decision. Academic attention at that time was rarely focused on contemporary literary production, though that was to change. The issue duly appeared in 1977, and was an important factor in getting the sort of writing that we and other small, independent presses were promoting and publishing recognised in the universities, and the incorporation of at least some of it onto the syllabuses.

Book launches were still not that common: there had not been that many books being initiated in Australia. The Wild & Woolley launches that Pat and I organised were designed to promote our titles, not just to assuage authorial vanity. When they were held, media people used to turn up: this was before everyone got jaded with too many things to go to. We splashed copies of books around: this was before the habit of using launches as a way to sell books. They soon became wilder and woollier and probably tended to get out of control. They might even have been counter-effective, as people afterwards desperately tried to repress embarrassing memories of what they had got up to at the event, and so suppressed any memory of the book being launched. I don't know why *Deep Throat* was screening at one of them, except that it was in the Sydney Film Co-operative building, so there was some sort of available screen. Dal Stivens' paintings on the wall seemed like a good idea at the time when we launched his book, even though one got damaged. But they were good parties, collecting a mix of young activists from the anti-war movement, the women's movement, gay rights, the old libertarians, the left, the dope freaks, comix aficionados, the *Tabloid Story* writers, emergent novelists, advocates of red bases on campus, filmmakers, performance artists, poets, painters, media people and journalists from that fertile moment of creativity.

And we got into all the ancillary promotional ideas. T-shirts with

Cobb's bufferoo on them, knitted woollen jumpers by Mary Murphett in multi-coloured rendition of the same.

'Why don't you guys publish some books instead of just doing T-shirts,' said Cheryl Adamson. Surreal Adamson, as Bob pronounced her name. That was before she became Cheryl Creatrix.

For a brief while we had Friday afternoon salons, inviting the writers along, but we had to stop them since they tended to end up in arguments with the poets. Or Pat did. In the end we decided it was best to stick to books, keep away from authors.

But the office, the warehouse, that was still a focal point. People visited. An editor from Routledge & Kegan Paul came by on a visit from England, looking to see if there was anything he might sign up. 'I think we'll take at least one title,' he assured us. We took him along to the inaugural opening of the Dolphin Embassy at the Yellow House in Kings Cross; this was an initiative by which we were all going to talk to dolphins. We got invited to all sorts of things back then. Nevertheless, he took my *Political Fictions*, a collection of essays on the novel and politics he published in 1980. I think Pat was relieved, it saved us from having to publish something as academic as that.

We had taken on distributing Fremantle Arts Centre Press, and their rep called in, a rather scatty old lady, as she seemed to me, but that was partly her rather English manner. Pat seemed to relate to her, though I couldn't. It was Elizabeth Jolley, before the celebrity her novels achieved for her; though I could never relate to the novels, either. And then there was Jim Haynes, an American who had run the Traverse theatre in Edinburgh and *Screw* magazine in Holland, passing by on a visit. Shar Adams who was working for us by this stage had known him in Amsterdam. Years later I picked up a copy of his memoirs in a remainder shop and was delighted to find it was dedicated to me and Pat, along with, I seem to remember, Bianca and Mick Jagger, Princess Margaret, Gore Vidal, Allen Ginsberg and a couple of thousand others of his closest and dearest friends. It deserves to be in the *Guinness Book of Records* for the most extensive dedication to date.

It was a scene. And a net. Or maybe a line. Decades later, when I stood down from the chair of the New South Wales Writers' Centre, Pat advised me to stay on the committee.

'It's a good fishing spot, you don't give it up,' she said.

I had never really thought about these things, and if the idea surfaced I rejected it as somehow improper. I had the idealistic 1960s vision that such things were wrong, advancement should be on merit, not connections. The meritocratic years. I believed it. Those of us without family or school or upper-class connections all believed it. What else could we believe? So there I was, all idiotic idealism.

Maybe at another level my autonomic nervous system disregarded what I felt I believed and manipulated me into position. Because publishing was a great position. I had never realised how great. I had always wanted the literary life. Undergraduate life in that regard had been a disappointment. I'd edited *Isis*, sure. But my hopes of a world of Audens and Isherwoods, of Beats and Angry Young Men, all working together creatively, were disappointed. In Sydney, however, I had found a literary world, and Wild & Woolley was a part of it.

The media were supportive. They were printing stories in the press. It was a new story. This was the cultural revival everyone had announced. This was the evidence that was needed. The books were reviewed. The women's magazines ran excerpts, interviews. I remember a visiting German writer being amazed to find us written up in *Cosmopolitan* and *Cleo* and *Pol* and *Vogue*. We were on radio, even television. It was all an endless blur, hype, and enthusiasm. We didn't take any of it terribly seriously, it was all fun, parties and launches and publicity and readings and radio and sex and drugs and rock 'n' roll.

I had got into publishing in recoil from the remorseless political preoccupations of the anti-war movement. I had wanted to escape back into literature. Now it was publishing that politicised me even further. Observing at close hand the business practices of the book trade, the whole practice of capitalism, the continual moves to remove competition and achieve market dominance, the production of commodities for sale rather than for use or value, was an education. At the same time I was publishing Jack Lindsay and *The Radical Reader* and reading further in left-wing writing and commentary – Jack London, William Morris, Christopher Hill. It all shifted me inexorably further left, at a time when the right was mobilising for its counter-revolution. Probably not the best timing from a career point of view. Not much fun, either, in the ensuing years. I started writing articles about the publishing industry and the problems for literature in Australia. By the end of the decade I calculated I had published a dozen such pieces, increasingly strident. I don't think they endeared me to the industry.

We were always trying new strategies. In 1978 Pat decided to raise our image in the marketplace. She decided we would change format and produce a batch of mass-market size paperbacks, with four-colour covers. No more small press style.

'Why small?' that cheerful old bookman Walter Stone of Wentworth Press, our first printer, would always complain. 'Why call yourselves small?'

Pat had taken his advice to heart. We would go for the appearance of mass-market titles. Pocket book format. Large runs to get a lower unit cost. It seemed best to experiment with a book of my own, in case the experiment failed. Pat found a co-publisher in New Zealand, John McIndoe, which helped raise the print run.

I had put together stories that had been excised from my first UQP collection, and others not offered to them in their second collection,

The West Midland Underground, because of their ongoing refusal of overtly sexual material. I had given a selection to a French printer in Sydney who had typeset some issues of *Tabloid Story* and had done an underground collection of three of Moorhouse's stories that he and Frank had deemed risqué. It was now out of print and I suggested to Frank that Wild & Woolley could reissue it. Frank had incorporated the stories into his *Tales of Mystery and Romance*, significantly revising the dialogue, his protagonist now getting the better lines. I thought a reissue of the original text might be interesting. Scholarly variants and all that. In part this was a gesture of rapprochement, an attempt to restore our former friendship.

For a number of years Frank and I had had a productive literary alliance. Like the two parts of a pantomime horse, Martin Johnston remarked in the *Sydney Morning Herald*. Laurie Duggan even suggested that my *Aspects of the Dying Process* and Frank's south coast collection, *The Electrical Experience*, should have a shared title, *Aspects of the Dairying Process*. When I told Frank that I was going to meet Pat in California, he said he would be in the USA at the same time and asked where I was staying so that he and Don Anderson and Sandra Levy could meet up with me there. My idea of California was the new alternative world of hippies and protest, of sex and drugs and rock'n'roll, that Pat had described so enticingly. I had no wish to transport the tone-deaf, alcohol fuelled, libertarian milieu of Balmain to Los Angeles.

Vicki Viidikas incited my resistance. 'Don't flipping tell him, I wouldn't.'

If I'd left it at that all might have been well. But I didn't. I wrote a letter spelling out my position. And for good measure added some further, simmering resentments, like, since I'd reviewed one of his books, why didn't he review one of mine. And so on.

And that was the end of a beautiful friendship. When I phoned him on my return Frank was decidedly chill. He declined invitations to meet for lunch, for drinks, for old times' sake. And he declined the offer to republish his underground collection.

Meanwhile nothing had happened in terms of the publication of my own stories.

'Why give them to someone else?' Pat complained.

So I put them together with some more I had not collected, and assembled *The Phallic Forest*. Sex was reputed to sell books, so with a title like that, maybe we could exploit the mass-market format and make some significant sales. We used the same – or similar – cover lettering on *The Phallic Forest* as UQP's edition of my *Living Together*, which was now in its third printing. Brand identification. By the author of *Living Together* and *The Short Story Embassy*. We used the author photograph of me that *Cosmopolitan* had used in its Bachelor of the Month feature, and credited *Cosmopolitan*. Celebrity. 'We should get you on *Celebrity Squares*,' Pat said. I realised with a shock she was serious. And we made the book a movie tie-in, too. A couple of years earlier the director Kit

Guyatt and I had made a movie of 'The Phallic Forest', which we toured as a double-bill with Phil Noyce's twin-screen documentary *Good Afternoon*. *The Phallic Forest* had got a fair bit of attention, not only from the press. We announced in the blurb: 'The title story was made into a short movie and its screening at the Melbourne Film Co-op caused raids and prosecution.' It had been a black-and-white movie and we couldn't find a suitable still for the cover, so Pat got a colour photo of a naked couple from Wes Stacey. Unfortunately a lot of shops refused to stock a book with naked people on the cover. Another lesson in marketing. The female lead, Victoria Anoux, recalls in her memoir *Losing Alexandria* (published under her married name, Victoria Thompson) that Patrick White was particularly taken by the movie. She told me that when Patrick and Manoly were in New York, Patrick sent her a card of a Rousseau painting of a nude nesting in a lush forest. He wrote on the back that it reminded him of *The Phallic Forest*. Had Pat and I known, we would certainly have splashed that endorsement around.

After nineteen issues, I finally extricated myself from *Tabloid Story*. Moorhouse had left it quite early on. Brian Kiernan had come to Sydney and been replaced as Melbourne editor by Colin Talbot. Carl Harrison-Ford and Damien White had been replaced by Pat as managing editor for the last dozen issues. But Pat and I had more than enough to do with Wild & Woolley, so we now handed *Tabloid Story* over to a team of Melbourne editors. We decided to commemorate it with an anthology from its first series. It had been an important breakthrough magazine, a stimulus in the renaissance of the Australian short story in the 1970s. It seemed worth memorialising something of what it had achieved. And it had product recognition. So we told ourselves. We featured stories by Peter Carey, Vicki Viidikas, Dal Stivens, Antigone Kefala, Murray Bail, Christine Townend, Peter Mathers, Carol Novack, Laurie Clancy, John (now Josie) Emery, Kris Hemensley, Rudi Krausmann, Bill Beard, Colin Talbot, Frank Moorhouse, Carmel Kelly, myself and many more. I wrote an afterword recording the magazine's history, expanded from a piece I had written for *New Journalist*. This would be the second mass-market title. We called it *The Tabloid Story Pocket Book*. Simon & Schuster had already appropriated the Australian kangaroo for their pocket book logo, so Paul Worsted drew a Penguin with a saw-edged beak for the cover. I couldn't work out whether it was meant to look predatory or defiant or punch drunk. It's an angry penguin, Pat explained.

And for the third mass-market title we decided on a dope book. Dope books might sell, even if short stories might not. I had stumbled across a nineteenth-century book on growing cannabis in Australia, *The Culture and Management of Hemp* by Francis Campbell, a doctor at the Tarban Creek asylum and friend of the Balmain literary patron Nicol Drysdale Stenhouse – the latter a friend of Thomas De Quincey, the Opium Eater. We reprinted Campbell's text, together with an account of its author that I wrote, incorporated the old *All About Grass* pamphlet, originally Dave Fleming's *The Complete Guide to Growing Marijuana*, further revised and expanded, and added a few other odds and ends the editor, Richard Crabtree, assembled. It all bulked out to a reasonable size book. But our costing was thrown when we were refused the book bounty subsidy on the grounds of subject matter. No court case, no conviction for anything, just the withholding of money. We went ahead, anyway.

But unless you have the huge distribution organisation of a media conglomerate, it is difficult to get mass-market sales; you have to print a lot of copies to get a low unit cost, but it is difficult to sell enough of them to make the scheme work profitably. It is safer to stick in a higher priced niche market, with more of a margin on which you can, possibly, survive.

In a further attempt to orient the publishing programme in a more profit-oriented direction, Pat did a couple of books in our cartoon and comix large format series that were meant to prove a commercial success. But to make a book a commercial success you have to invest a lot of time and money in it, you have to print a large number of copies to enable a profit to be made, and that requires a significant financial outlay; and if it isn't a success, then you can lose a lot of money. Bob Gould suggested we publish a collection of Bruce Petty's cartoons from the *Age*, and we did it as *The Petty Age* in 1978. Petty had earlier been a cartoonist on the *Australian*. The problem with the *Age* was that it was hardly seen in Sydney. But Petty was still well-known, and had a following. Pat did a large print run and negotiated with a commercial distributor, Gordon & Gotch, to handle it. They demanded an exclusive contract, so we could not supply the title ourselves. That meant that a number of our regular, independent booksellers, who got good results with our books, but did not have accounts with Gordon & Gotch, could not obtain it. Worse than that, the distributors scaled out copies around Australia to country towns and other places that had never heard of Petty, or if they had, didn't like him. They went out sale or return. The returns were huge.

Then in 1980 there was the collection of Cobb's colour art, *Colourvision*. It was expensive to produce, involved disputes with the printer over colour registration, and likewise didn't do that well.

It must have been around this time that Peter Corris brought over the first of his Cliff Hardy private eye novels. I was no longer involved in the company and never saw the manuscript and Pat was not taking on new fiction. A missed opportunity. But the fiction list wasn't covering its costs. It had to come to an end.

We had shown the way. One way, anyway. Come the 1980s the local branches of the multinationals began initiating Australian fiction for the first time on a significant and sustained scale. Previously they had done the occasional hard cover title and once in a while a paperback reprint. Now they began following the example of UQP, Outback and Wild & Woolley, and publishing new fiction directly into paperback. They found there was a market there.

In 1978 I received a year's fellowship from the Literature Board. I had asked for three, but this was all I got; all I ever got, all I've ever had. I was increasingly dissatisfied with the university. I wanted to break away, and write. But travelling through Britain and the USA I found that the small presses I had encountered in 1974 and 1975 and 1976 were now all struggling, the independent writers I had met were all looking for institutional shelter. It didn't seem like a good time to leave the university and try and live as a writer. The world was changing. Soon Mrs Thatcher became prime minister of Britain, Ronald Reagan president of the USA.

Through the seventies I had operated on the principle of do everything, take up every offer. Insofar as there was any principle behind this, it was that some sort of survival of the fittest process would operate and the worthwhile activities would be revealed and would endure. I'm not sure that is quite what happened.

I was doing too much. I tried to cut down on my activities and conserve some energy. Apart from university, my full-time job, I was writing fiction. I was writing academic essays too, based on my teaching. I ceased editing *Tabloid Story* but I was still editing UQP's Asian and

Pacific Writing series. I resigned from the Literature Board. I stopped assessing scripts for the Australian Film Commission. I stopped reviewing books for the press, though I still reviewed for academic journals and the occasional literary magazine. I was writing a column for *Nation Review*, though that too came to an end. All in all I was feeling stressed and exhausted.

Pat looked at the business grimly. There was no way we could go on as we were. We were not actually losing money. The distribution business brought in enough regular income to cover the bills. But the Australian literary publishing was barely profitable. It broke even, as I had hoped. But it was not generating enough surplus to support Pat and pay staff.

It was always a financial struggle. Pat figured that since Wild & Woolley came at the end of the alphabet, bookshops ran out of money before they got around to paying our accounts. Eventually, when together with Ian and Sally Hoyle and Shar Adams she set up a distribution arm, she called it AllBooks to get us at the top of the list. I'm not sure this alphabetical strategy made much difference.

But, as Pat explains further: 'The reason I started AllBooks (with Shar, Ian and Sally) was that Book People of Australia lost Wild and Woolley about $6000 in moneys they owed us for distributing our books (a deal that Morry Schwartz set up) and I, on my return from three months in the US running about shops selling Wild & Woolley books, said, well, if they can lose $6000 for me, I could lose it too, but at least I'll know where it's gone.'

In 1980 Pat opted for making a full-on bid for commercial success. She proposed hiring a fleet of Escort vans for an enlarged distribution program. Could it have been twelve of them?

I refused to sign the lease agreement. I recognised the problem. I could see where she wanted to go. But I wanted to withdraw back into my writing, put that in primary place, and disentangle myself from the mass of activities I was involved with.

I was no longer active in the company when the new warehouse in the old wool building in Kent Street burned down one weekend. Wild & Woolley had been jointly leasing the premises with Ian and Sally Hoyle's Wobbledagger for their shared AllBooks Distribution. I got a phone call, went down to the burned-out site, soggy spy books and homosexual literature floating down the gutters, as the *Sun-Herald* put it. Everything smelled of eucalyptus. Possibly an exploding eucalyptus distiller on level four caused the fire. We never found out. We had a lugubrious lunch in the old Malaya restaurant near Central station. Roger Barnes, our printer, was there; Bob Gould the bookseller; Marius Webb from ABC radio 2JJ; Pat, and myself. I can't remember what was said. It was beyond words.

One morning in the early 1980s Roger Barnes from Southwood Press phoned. He and his wife Sylvia Hale were running their own publishing company, Hale & Iremonger, which they set up with John Iremonger who had now gone to Allen & Unwin. Hale & Iremonger's list had initially been one of political, social and historical issues. Now Roger phoned me to say they were thinking of publishing fiction.

'A great idea,' I assured him. 'Do you want a manuscript?'

'Hold on, hold on,' he said.

I put the copy of *Pacific Highway* back down and held on.

'So what do you think?' he asked.

I told him what I thought. A brilliant proposal, something he should definitely do, lots of good material around I could put him onto, guaranteed to get Literature Board subsidies. If you could face filling out the application forms and the acquittals.

Maybe twenty minutes later he phoned again.

'If it's such a great idea,' he said, 'why are you and Pat not publishing fiction anymore?'

'Ah well,' I said, 'ah, well.'

'Cash flow,' I might have added. Or explained that Pat wanted to go mass-market.

'Anyway, you've got the printery, you can cut costs that way, printing your own books.'

He grunted.

But he did it. He took *Pacific Highway* and a book by his next-door neighbour, Gerard Windsor, and a collection of stories by Peter Shrubb, a colleague of mine who had held a Stanford creative writing fellowship decades earlier, published in the *New Yorker*, and vanished from view. I let Roger negotiate that one, since Peter and I had disagreed vigorously about the Vietnam war and I felt he would have been suspicious of any approach from me.

With Hale & Iremonger developing a literary list, I was able to move some of the Wild & Woolley stable across to them, rather than leaving our authors abandoned. In due course Hale & Iremonger published Vicki Viidikas, Nigel Roberts, Billy Jones, Rudi Krausmann and Robert Adamson as well as my *Pacific Highway*, *Reading the Signs* and a selection of *Stories by Marcus Clarke* that I introduced.

Bob Adamson had ended up spending the Prism Poets subsidy before he had published David Brooks' poems, which he had committed to. I persuaded Roger to take that book on and extricate Bob from some of his difficulties. He did so, and at the same time mysteriously discovered a batch of unbound sheets of Bob's magnificent, expensive, large format book of poems, *Cross the Border*, which Southwood had printed for Prism a year or so earlier. Bob and Roger fiddled around with the cover, a two-panel construct by Brett Whiteley and Gary Shead, got the panels in the correct order this time, and reissued it from Hale & Iremonger.

Another book I alerted Roger to was Martin Johnston's novel *Cicada Gambit*. I hadn't searched it out for Wild & Woolley because Martin's aesthetic was too Nabokovian for my taste, chess games, Borges, that sort of thing. But Roger published it, and a volume of Martin's poems. Martin was one of the few writers ever to come up and thank me for having got him published. Don'o Kim's novel *The Chinaman* was another title I put Hale & Iremonger's way. I also helped out on the slush pile once in a while, sifting through a cardboard box of unsolicited manuscripts from which I picked out the first of Ross Fitzgerald's Clinton Everest campus novels.

'This is awful,' I said, 'but it will sell. It's like Tom Sharpe,' I told Roger.

Awful in the sense that it offended most proprieties and decencies, all moderation and restraint, elegance or subtlety. And how appropriate for writing about university life.

And after Transworld picked the series up it did sell, doing especially well in Britain and South Africa.

Roger also bound up some left-over sheets of Lloyd Ross's *William Lane and the Australian Labor Movement*, which had been sitting in a shed since the 1930s, and which Lloyd Ross told me about in the course of my researches for *The Paraguayan Experiment*. And he rebound some remaindered copies of my *Political Fictions* that Pat had bought from Routledge & Kegan Paul and given to me, putting them under the Hale & Iremonger imprint. Years later whoever it was who had taken over Routledge billed Pat for them and she billed me.

The dispute meant finding a solicitor who sorted it all out. This was when I was billed for all those copies I had taken from the warehouse, too.

'That's it,' I said. 'I'll give up publishing now.'

'You won't,' the solicitor assured me.

Adamson's *New Poetry* had collapsed into a financial morass. The grant money had been spent. I managed to raise $1000 from the university through the professor of Australian Literature, Dame Leonie Kramer. Both Bob and I endlessly received through the mail poems, translations and stories from writers we had met or corresponded with around the world. We gathered the scattered material and pretty well had another issue of the magazine. A few specific invitations completed it and we had a new issue to satisfy Bob's obligations to the Literature Board.

Then Bob and I tried to get Roger to publish the magazine in future, and we took *New Poetry's* IBM Composer across to him; we never saw it again. Roger was interested and a couple of issues were printed. Tim Thorne and Terry Gillmore somehow came in as guest editors and they took some excerpts from Vicki Viidikas' new novel in manuscript, *Kali and the Dung Beetle* – though they used a rather eccentric selection of uncharacteristically historical and contextual material rather than fiction, it seemed to Bob and me. Vicki threatened to sue, I forget on what grounds. But there were worse problems. The debts to various previous printers and the various legal complexities were such that Roger decided not to proceed with the idea of publishing the magazine.

'Run it as a tax loss,' we exhorted him.

He looked at us in bemused puzzlement and explained patiently that you have to be making a profit somewhere in order to run something as a tax loss. Fair enough. So, 1983, that was the end of an era, and an excellent magazine ceased to appear. We never got the Composer back. Rudi Krausmann's *Aspect* magazine ceased not long afterwards, in debt for its printing to Roger. Phil Roberts packed it all in around this time, too, gave up his university lectureship and Island Press and went back to North America where he wrote a couple of very successful books on how to read poetry for Penguin's educational list.

Meanwhile Pat expanded the Wild & Woolley import and distribution business, AllBooks. In a submission to the 2008 inquiry into copyright restrictions on the parallel importing of books she described what happened.

'We represented about 60 publishers and held stocks of each book in print. In 1986, computers were just coming into use. Bar codes were still in the future. Computer stock control was on the horizon.

'In 1990, we had irrefutable evidence that one of our major customers was importing books in which we had the exclusive Australian licence. We had purchased the stocks from California, we had spent considerable amounts of money publicising the titles and authors, we had supplied review copies at no costs to the media, and our sales representatives called monthly to check supplies and restock titles.

'The evidence came to us because we were asked to load our stockholding data onto the bookseller's new computer system. They had just put in a computerised stock control system. And there, on the computer, Wild & Woolley was shown as the last preferred supplier: two US wholesalers were ranked over us, because buying books from them would cost less.

'That bookseller sold the books at the same price. They made a greater margin on the books, which they imported illegally, than they made on the books which they bought from us. They didn't lower the prices to their customers. The books weren't cheaper. They ripped off their customers.

'They ripped us off, too. Because we had made the investment in stock, we had a warehouse stacked with small and large quantities of books, we had full time staff, cars, and overheads, and we paid Australian tax.

'Of course I took legal advice but the fee to mount and run a case, which might have included flying the author (a practical impossibility because he was a well known, undependable drunk) to Australia to give evidence, was more than I could risk. Instead, I shut down AllBooks Distribution.'

Over the years Australian governments have consistently disadvantaged books and writers. The movie industry had its tax incentive schemes for investors. Television had its quota of local content. Computers were promised for every senior school student. In contrast the book industry suffered from one piece of negative legislation after another.

GST is the notorious example. The 10 per cent goods and services tax on the retail price of books and magazines increased the price to the consumer of items that were already more expensive than the identical product in the USA or UK. It also added a further burden to small, independent Australian publishers and booksellers. Large global corporations can afford to introduce systems and to employ accountants and auditors to service their widespread activities. But the one- or two- person small presses, little magazines or independent bookshops struggle to find the time, energy, expertise or finance to handle the paperwork of quarterly reporting. In Britain books are exempt from VAT, value added tax, the equivalent of GST. But not in Australia.

The abolition of retail price maintenance was achieved decades ago. This was presented as a great liberation for the consumer. Instead of books having to be sold at a price nominated by the publisher, they could now be sold at any price. Everything would be competitive and cheaper. It wasn't, it isn't. A handful of nominated bestsellers are now routinely discounted each month by the bookselling chains and the supermarkets. Small independent booksellers cannot move the volume of stock required to be given discount prices by the publishers, so they inevitably lose market share.

Authors similarly lose out, unless they have written one of the handful of discounted titles. The abolition of retail price maintenance in the UK resulted in a handful of best sellers being sold considerably more cheaply, while the price of other titles rose by 10 to 15 per cent (£1 a book on average) and their sales dropped. Retail price maintenance is still observed in Germany. But not in Australia.

For years Australia Post offered a concessional printed matter postage rate, significantly lower than parcel post. But the government authorised the abolition of this category. It is now ridiculously expensive to mail a book as a gift. And it is punitively expensive for small publishers who rely on the postal service for distribution. The global conglomerates can afford alternatives like contracts with couriers and trucking companies. Once again the smaller independent Australian publishers and booksellers are penalised. And the consumer suffers, as the bookseller passes on the postal cost to the consumer. The USA still retains preferential printed matter rates. But not Australia.

Printing is expensive in Australia. Far more expensive than in the USA, for instance, let alone Asia. For a while a generous book bounty scheme subsidised the cost of printing in Australia, in an effort to discourage publishers from printing offshore. This has now been abolished. The free trade anti-protection lobbies have had their way. The consequence is that Australian manufactured books are generally at a disadvantage in terms of production costs compared with those imported from USA or UK publishers. As for printing overseas, this is rarely cost effective for small runs, so small presses, literary fiction, minority interest titles hardly benefit from any lower prices available.

Once again Australian independent publishers, writers and readers suffer.

The free trade lobbyists have also seen the end of the closed market, by which UK or USA publishers nominated an official agent for their books in Australia. Booksellers had to order from the Australian supplier and could not purchase directly from overseas wholesalers or distributors. This was perceived as a colonialist or imperialist restraint of trade, and abolished by governmental decree. But it had its positive aspects. When we set up Wild & Woolley to publish new Australian writing, we knew our sales would be comparatively small. We maintained our cash flow by importing books from the USA and the UK. We stocked the complete lists of City Lights, New Directions and Black Sparrow, and for the first time ever their books were all widely distributed throughout Australia. Then governmental legislation abolished the closed market. Our business became unviable as bookshops purchased directly from overseas. We ceased to publish new Australian fiction, poetry and essays. And the City Lights, New Directions and Black Sparrow titles vanished from all but a handful of specialist bookshops – and even then, only their lead titles were stocked.

There were good arguments for all these legislative decisions. Cumulatively, however, they worked against the interests of Australian writers, readers, publishers and booksellers And we still don't have a genuine free market in books, copyright deals preventing the importing of overseas editions that sell for half the price of the identical book published under an Australian imprint. Unless you buy them on-line from overseas – which of course further undermines the local retailers. To be fair, there have been positive governmental initiatives like Public and Education Lending Right, the Copyright Agency and the Literature Board of the Australia Council. Though these are not without their critics. And whatever their strengths, they do not compensate for the damage done by those other pieces of decision making.

In the changed commercial and legislative environment, Pat survived by abandoning distribution and moving Wild & Woolley and a sister imprint Fast Books into subsidy publishing, specialising in family histories, memoirs, short run books. It was a pioneering, innovatory and successful development, and fulfilled an increasing demand.

Pat and I lost track of each other for a time, and then in the mid-1990s we met again when she came onto the committee of the New South Wales Writers' Centre. Naturally we cooked up a scheme for the Centre to program a small press, independent and self- publishers' book fair. It ran as an annual event for the next decade.

At some point early in the new century I offered her a manuscript as a guinea-pig for a new publishing scheme she had in mind. There was supposed to be some money available to help publishers in compensation for the introduction of GST on books. A lot of time was wasted until it emerged that the money was not there. Not for us, anyway.

I had offered her my novel about the university, *Academia Nuts*. Bob Adamson had announced he was going to publish it with Paper Back Press, which by this stage had found a wealthy partner. But negotiations had broken down between Bob and my agent. Pat came to my rescue. And although the new scheme had come to nothing, she still went ahead.

'I'll publish you,' she said. 'For all that money you put in to start Wild & Woolley.'

A bit later the offer had changed to, 'I'll publish you in exchange for your share-holding in Wild & Woolley'.

I didn't even know I had any shares.

'Sure,' I said.

So she published me. Again. The year was 2002, for the record.

And then the complimentary copies of *Academia Nuts* I was mailing round the world through the departmental mail at university were impounded. I discovered them a month later when I was asked what research grant they were to be billed to. I had thought that sending a recent publication to my international peers was an appropriate thing to do. They weren't even review copies; just copies to academics. Academics who moonlighted as novelists or cultural critics or editors or publishers, maybe, but still academics. I had assumed as an emeritus professor I had mail rights, or if not rights, at least privileges. Clearly not.

I drove the copies across to Pat in Glebe, and asked her would she mail these as well as the review copies. She agreed to, on certain conditions. The first edition was nearly sold out and she wanted to make some alterations before she reprinted: she proposed changing the order of the opening episodes and she demanded a new chapter for a new ending. She suggested I should write one about the mail impounding.

There had already been a change of cover after Pat had decided she didn't like the appearance of the advance copies; she issued a press release stating that they had too much cholesterol in them, which got us some valuable publicity.

Publishers' suggestions for revisions are always a bit worrying to a writer, but variant editions are a splendid thing for collectors and for attracting scholarly attention. They are the very stuff of scholarly discourse and they ensure a place in the bibliographies. Academic careers have been built on noting such revisions and discrepancies.

I agreed. Who was I to refuse a second edition? So we did it.

Then in 2010 Pat told me she had retired and closed the business down.

Meanwhile I had got involved in a new publishing venture, Press On…

ILLUSTRATIONS

3 Pat Woolley at the Chippendale office in 1978, photograph by Philip du Rhone.

22, 23 The Buffaroo, Wild & Woolley's mascot, © Ron Cobb. All rights reserved, used with permission of Wild & Woolley, Sydney.

37 The author in the Wild & Woolley warehouse in Chippendale.

45 The author, Pat Woolley, Lawrence Ferlinghetti and an unidentified friend at City Lights bookshop, San Francisco, 1973.

66 The first issue of *Tabloid Story*, 1972.

97 The Chippendale office from 1975–1978. Ron Cobb has just painted the name on the front. Robin Love stands to his side. The Bega dry cleaner's van is also alongside.

103 The author with poets outside the Woolley Building at Sydney University, left to right: Chris Edwards, Tom Thompson, Robert Adamson, Nigel Roberts, Lyndy Abraham, Tim Thorne, Michael Wilding, Robert Duncan (kneeling).

120 Michael and Pat, Breakfast of Champions, San Francisco, 1973.

ACKNOWLEDGEMENTS

Parts of this memoir have appeared in the *Australian*, *Weekend Australian*, *Sydney Morning Herald*, *Newswrite* and *Wet Ink*.

Thanks to Pat Woolley, Nicholas Pounder and Philip du Rhone for their help in sourcing photographs; and to Carl Harrison-Ford for his copy-editing of the text.

This project has been assisted by the Commonwealth Government through the Australia Council, its arts funding and advisory body.

BIOGRAPHICAL NOTE

Michael Wilding has published some fifty books including novels, literary criticism, and collections of essays and short stories. He co-edited the magazine *Tabloid Story*, and co-founded the publishing houses Wild & Woolley and Paperbark Press. He has taught at the Universities of California (Santa Barbara), Birmingham and Sydney, where he is now Emeritus Professor. He is a former *Cosmopolitan* Bachelor of the Month, Fellow of the Australian Academy of the Humanities, and Chair of the NSW Writers' Centre.

A detailed list of Michael Wilding's publications can be found at www.michael-wilding.com